Happiness Skills

based on Positive Psychology

Michaela Avlund MSc is a Positive Psychologist. She has given classes and workshops in various parts of Ireland over the past 10 years. She specialises in working with groups or individuals around Happiness Skills and is currently working with Transition Year students. She is a regular speaker at the bi-annual Mind, Body, Spirit and Yoga Festival in the RDS in Dublin. She lives in a community in Wicklow dedicated to supporting people in the pursuit of physical, mental and spiritual well-being. She has written and co-produced two Self-confidence and Relationship DVDs which have been used in Secondary schools all over Ireland. The Independent printed her '15 tips to Happiness' interview in March 2015. She loves walking and cycling on country roads around counties Wicklow and Kildare but also leads groups in various parts of Ireland for Positive Psychology, Creative Writing and Sound Therapy Getaways.

Happiness Skills

based on Positive Psychology

Michaela Avlund

Published in 2015 by SOL Productions

Enquiries to:
SOL Productions
Quarantine Hill
Wicklow Town
michaela@HappinessSkills.ie

ISBN: 190171226-5

Illustrations © Ken Kelly 2015
colorman@me.com

This copy is printed by
LetsPrint.ie

13th May 2017

To Sonya
Love always.
Mum xox

To everyone who wishes to grow
or support others
in lasting well-being and happiness.

This book is dedicated
to
Annie and Bent Avlund

My mum Annie who in spite of childhood traumas did everything in her power to keep her six children healthy physically and spiritually. She searched for the positive truth and had nothing but encouragement for me and my siblings in spite of her own mental torments.

My dad Bent introduced me to psychology and the importance of love. He saved me at a confusing time in my youth by sharing his mantra 'Everything works for good for those who love Goodness', something I have personally experienced throughout my life to be true.

Acknowledgements

This book has been inspired by the many participants in my workshops and classes over the past years, individuals who have welcomed my material and these skills as super encouraging and relevant to everyday living.

I truly stand on the shoulders of giants. So I wish to thank the many positive psychologists who through their research are supporting all my personal discoveries of how to be happy and stay well in this often confusing and difficult world.

Martin Seligman for his leadership in this area, Barbara Fredrickson for her research on our need for positive emotions. Dr Robert Emmons for his dedication to exploring the benefit of gratitude in all walks of life. Dr Richard Davidson for his amazing break-through research on our ability to create a positive brain environment which can change our lives to optimism and 'can-do' living.

I wish to thank Dr James Pennebaker for sharing the post-traumatic writing process that enables people to heal from hurtful experiences. Martin Seligman and Christopher Peterson for their work on character strengths which encourages us to focus on the strengths that energise us and pursue a life that we love.

I wish to thank Kristin Neff for her emphasis on self-compassion and self-minding. Dr David Hamilton for his exploration of the vagus-nerve and how we can positively affect our immune system.

I wish to thank Dr Illona Boniwell for setting up the master degree in applied positive psychology which I completed in London. For the encouragement of the lecturers there Kate Heffernan and co-students who shared my enthusiasm for bringing Happiness skills into mainstream teaching in Ireland.

I wish to thank the Danish trust that sponsored my studies, the Wicklow VEC and the Irish mature student scheme that enabled me to take a social care degree in Carlow. The lecturers in St. Patrick's Carlow college who acknowledged my skills and helped me to build on these.

I wish to thank the generous individuals who shared their stories with me of how they used particular happiness skills that were crucial to their positive developments and well-being. I wish to thank Ken Kelly for his amazing illustrations.

I wish to thank the community I live in for the continual support and encouragement, not only to stay healthy but for giving me the time out to write this book. For the help in accessing sponsorship for studying and publishing this book.

On a personal level I wish to thank Harry Parkinson for his continual availability to discuss and edit the contents, and for his healing sound therapy. Torhild Oien for her professional advice and encouragement. Vera Walsh for her positive participation and encouragement. Bernard Kirby and Maura Power for their time and comments. Seamus Byrne for his professional publishing advice, Veronica O'Reilly for her marketing advice, Gabrielle Kirby for her inspiration and Paul Diamond for helping everything to run smoothly.

I wish to thank the many fellow catholics who have shown their delight at the title of this book and wished me good luck.

A special thank you to my friend Donal and family for the use of a quiet haven away from all distractions where I could give my total attention to the book. To Donal, my 'fitness' companion in walking and cycling on country roads around beautiful Ireland, helping me stay connected to nature. Gratitude also to my sister Eva, my brothers, and my nieces and nephew who all encouraged and supported me.

Finally, the biggest gratitude of all to God the Creator and protector of beauty and goodness who lives inside each one of us and to whom I owe everything.

CONTENTS

INTRODUCTION

WHY HAPPINESS SKILLS?

It can be quite a journey to get to the place within ourselves where we believe it is possible to personally contribute something worthwhile in the lives of others and in society whilst also increasing our own happiness and well-being.

My own journey started when I was 15 years old and my mum had a mental breakdown. Whilst searching for ways to cope and find meaning with it all I became quite spiritually aware and eventually joined an unusual monastic community which was dedicated to seeing God's goodness in everything. However, I still felt there was something missing regarding the processing of negative feelings and thoughts that can be experienced by living in close proximity to others.

Psychology was helpful as it enabled me to identify and welcome anger as an important personal message pointing out to me what I felt deep down was truly important in life.

Anger can be a negative power but to me the discovery of my own anger was an enabling experience. Someone else might spark off our anger but when we treasure that moment rather than try to get away from it we can tap in to a greater knowledge of who we are and what we care deeply about.

I am angry but also sad when I hear of someone who takes their own life, especially a young person, because I see it as unnecessary. I am frustrated because I know that happiness and well-being is something everyone can create through a number of positive habits. I do not blame the individual or people around the person who took their own life, they more than likely did the best they knew how to support and love the person. However, I do blame our educational system for not including lifeskills training on an equal level to academic knowledge.

The research is clear: as individuals we cannot function properly, we cannot absorb new knowledge when we are stressed, emotionally upset, feeling down, bullied or disinterested in life. It is well overdue that we implement living skills teaching, that we give young people opportunities for developing well-being and happiness skills in an otherwise confusing and disempowering world that will drain our energy and crush our dreams without these skills.

This book presents a range of positive living skills that have worked for me and my students, the people I live with but more importantly for people in every corner of the world[1].

My mother, I believe would not have had to struggle with depression and anxiety for the rest of her days had she been taught and given an opportunity to practise these well-being skills earlier on in life. Being overly medicated she experienced the sideeffects that accompany medications. This is not a condemnation of drugs but we know so much more now of the personal power we have to change our brains.

Through brainscanning we can now see which parts of the brain are stimulated when we experience happiness and well-being. We can pin-point the type of thoughts that uplift us. We can observe how certain actions practised over only a few weeks activate feel-good hormones in our brains that energise, help us to trust more, to better focus and enjoy life.

Positive psychology specialises in the study of what we human beings do when we are happy, engaged and have found purpose in our lives. It has become clear that we can change our brain pathways and increase our zest for life by taking certain actions and making certain adjustments in our way of thinking.

We can create a successful and satisfying life way beyond our dreams. We can help people around us particularly the younger generation, provided we ourselves become role-models for well-being and happiness.

These well-being skills are small easily practised habits we can develop that change our brain environment and stimulate our feel good hormones dopamine and serotonin. These skills empower us to pursue a life that we can love and be proud of; they bring us to a higher level of honesty, fairness and genuine care for ourselves and all other living creatures in the universe. These lifeskills enable us to make a positive contribution in the world not at the expense of our own well-being but hand in hand with a flourishing and thriving personal existence.

This book presents seven areas of wellness skills easily developed. Some skills such as problem solving or assertiveness skills are useful in particular situations while other skills such as creating positive relationships, having selfkindness and being grateful empower our entire lives.

Each skill stands on its own, thus you can dip into this 'manual' at any place without prior knowledge. Each of the living skills presented has through research been shown to work really well for innumerable people. These are skills that I wish I would have known earlier in life in order to bring them to people who have ended up despairing and suicidal not realising that well-being and happiness lie within everyone's reach with a bit of encouragement and support.

We cannot choose for someone else. Each of us has a free choice whether to take on life enhancing and nourishing thinking and behaviour patterns. We each have the power to create a personal environment of peace, happiness and purpose within our minds and bodies that will guide us to choose optimism and care in everyday life and adverse situations.

This book shows how happiness and well-being are determined by the habits we choose to cultivate. You will find life-stories of people who have experienced adversity but used these life-skills to move beyond a life-crisis into lives full of well-being, happiness and hope. Specific **Brain Train** tasks will guide you to increase and permanently boost your happiness and care skills – provided you practise them!

By you taking responsibility for cultivating your own happiness and well-being you will not only discover a higher energy level and better health, but you will also become an inspiration for other people to do the same.

I wish you luck on this journey.

PLEASE NOTE: To protect confidentiality, the names of the people who share their well-being stories have been changed.

CHAPTER ONE

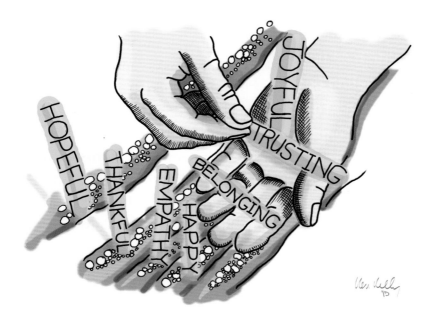

POSITIVE EMOTIONS AND GRATITUDE
Do we really need to feel good?

Feeling good is not a luxury, it is a necessity. Research clearly shows how often we are stressed and can burn ourselves out unless we proactively cultivate positive emotions.

Do we really need to feel good?

Feeling good can be underestimated as childish or naive, but feeling good is a deciding factor when it comes to our personal happiness and health.

I was brought up not to pay too much attention to my feelings. Life was more about fulfilling daily tasks and 'being good' rather than being happy and fulfilled. Then after a disappointment in a close relationship, someone I trusted asked me 'What do you want?' I suddenly realised that I had never really allowed myself to focus on my personal happiness.

I had supported other people's well-being but had not paid much attention to my personal aspirations and happiness.

Since then I have met numerous people who also find it difficult to allow themselves to pursue happiness for themselves. Pressures to be successful or liked can stop us from paying attention to the feel good factor in our lives.

Barbara Fredrickson[2] is an American professor who has researched this whole area of positive feelings and emotions. She discovered that positive emotions lead to high energy and vibrant health. When we feel good we also tend to be more generous and creative. We enjoy every part of our lives – even the challenges. Positive emotions build up our capacity to overcome negative experiences and fight off anxiety and depression.

In Europe and North America depression and anxiety is on the increase, starting at a younger age than ever before (WHO)[3]. Interviews with young pop stars who have an abundance of fame and money reveal that they often live in a deep state of depression and become

> Life is so much better when we feel good so why don't we just do what it takes to feel good?

chemically dependant on drugs to stimulate the feel good hormones in their bodies. While this works for a while, sooner or later it tears down personal confidence and enjoyment to know that one cannot get through the day without alcohol or drugs.

Cathal is one of the lucky ones who has survived years of dependency on alcohol and sometimes stronger drugs to deal with his negative feelings. He is thankful that he has found a healthier and more uplifting way of creating positive emotions as he is now a therapist who helps people to relax and enjoy better health. He explains;

I drank to numb the bad feelings but when you drink you numb everything, good and bad. I now realise that my negative feelings and thoughts are memories or a negative interpretation of what happened and not necessarily what other people experienced. I now know I have a choice how I view something and remember it.

Most people that have been on the road I have been on have lost everything. I still have a family, I still have the means of earning a living and I am grateful for that.

Of course we want to feel good, but sometimes life's chores and wounds seem to prevent us from exploring our potential. We may not realise how much power we have to create a wonderful life for ourselves.

Using our
Positive Management Centre

Scientists can now see what physically happens within our brains when we feel good and when we feel bad. Professor Richard Davidson has spent a lifetime investigating exactly what happens in the brain when we experience positive and negative emotions. He discovered a management centre at the very front of our brains called the Prefrontal Cortex. Here he noticed activity in the left or the right area according to whether we feel good or bad and according to whether we focus on positive or negative thoughts.

The amazing discovery is that we can choose which part of our brain to 'feed' and nourish. Whatever type of thoughts we focus on activate either the **Left management centre** (highlighted in green) or the **Right management centre** of the brain (highlighted in red). Why is this important?

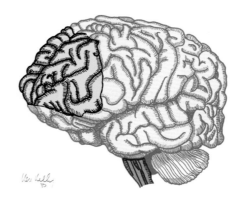

Unknown to ourselves we might automatically activate our negativity system. We human beings have a strong survival instinct and the constant stream of negative information from our surroundings activates our negativity bias. We need to counteract this overly activated survival system by deliberately nourishing the positivity home in our brains which will then produce greater well-being.

If we are not careful we keep activating the brain centre that leads to anxiety, worry and depression.

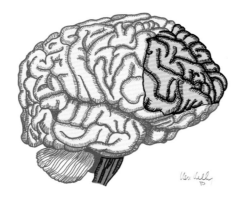

Our right pre-frontal cortex (R-PFC) which is situated on the right at the front of our brains, is the management centre which is activated by negative emotions and negative thoughts (red area).

This part of the brain is especially active when we feel aggressive, depressed or anxious. It is like a negative circuit that produces physical inactivity and isolation. This management centre is superactive in people who feel depressed, as negative thoughts and feelings intermingle and colour life as unsafe and meaningless.

A message is sent to the body that it is not worthwhile making an effort, that one cannot make a difference and that nothing will ever change for the better. Most people experience moments like this but if we are not careful these moments can extend and multiply and before we know it, we are stuck in a negative cycle. The danger is that too much focus is put on the negative part of life and little nourishment is given to the other side, which is linked to positive thoughts and emotions.

Here we see the small primal brain at the top of the spine called the amygdala (red dot) which activates negative brain activity.

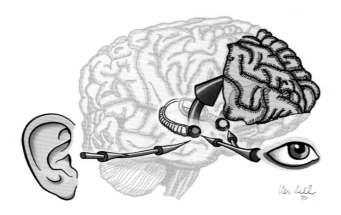

We see or hear something and if there is activity already in the R-PFC management centre which expects danger and difficulties, the Amygdala then alerts the body's defence system. Our whole interior gets ready for action.

The mouth gets dry, the heart beats faster, the digestive system is upset and we experience anxiety or restlessness. Our interior organs are now working at their minimal in order to allow the production of adrenaline, the 'fight or flight' response. Adrenaline gives us extra energy to either run away or defend ourselves against whatever it is we feel threatened by; even if it is all imaginary!

13

Our Minds and Bodies
tend to be in over-drive

Our nerve defense system tends to stay activated for much longer than is healthy or necessary.

We may not notice changes in our bodies, all we notice is that we are not feeling great a lot of the time; we are stressed and uncomfortable. These activated stress hormones prevent us from being creative and appreciative of the goodness in our lives.

It has become normal in our society to be bombarded with daily negative news of catastrophies from all over the world; of murders, accidents and deceptions at our own doorsteps. No one seems trustworthy any more, whatever efforts we make seem bound to fail due to all the odds against us; this is a natural conclusion from receiving a stream of ongoing negative news.

Even if we manage to avoid information overload our genetic wiring might also leave us disadvantaged. As a human race we have had to survive physical threats from wild animals, tribal attacks and severe climate changes. We are genetically hard-wired for survival.

14

On top of that, a great number of people might have had certain traumatic childhood or adolescent experiences. It is as if emotionally we are still back at the time when this bad or very upsetting experience took place, expecting it to possibly happen again.

> If we have not had a chance to process negative events in our lives and put them into a helpful perspective, it will darken our present experiences.

Cathal's little boy died only a few days after being born. Cathal did not have the ability to deal with this in a healthy way until later on when he had been treated for his addiction to drink and drugs:

When Neil died my dependency took on a whole new sinister level. I stopped communicating. I felt isolated inside and it was only after having a break-down and going into detox and recovery that I was able to view my life more objectively.

Eventually I realised that my son's short life was a gift, an opportunity to learn. I found that I could actually go back and access hope in the situation and come out with a new perspective.

Now I see all that I have experienced as a means to empathise and be of service. I am able to access deep feelings of empathy with people who have experienced sorrow in their lives.

Positive emotions calm our nervous system and boost our immune system[4].

In 1998 a new branch of psychology got funding to investigate what we human beings do when things go right for us, when we feel good, are healthy and feel happy.

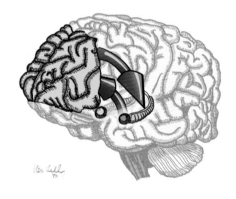

What scientists discovered was that when a person is well and happy there is a lot of activity in the front left management centre of the brain, the left pre-frontal cortex (L-PFC), which then slows down the Amygdala distress signals. When this positive activity is strong enough it signals to the Amygdala not to activate the defence system.

When there are activities in this left management centre (green area) the whole body works so much better. The hippocampus (the yellow area behind the amygdala) builds up long-term good memories which create an environment of relaxation in the brain and helps to activate the Vagus Nerve. The Vagus Nerve runs from the left management centre of the brain down to all the interior organs (left image below).

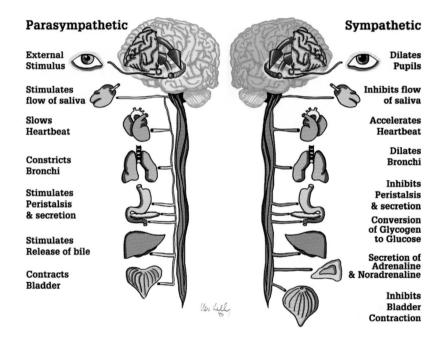

Parasympathetic

External Stimulus

Stimulates flow of saliva

Slows Heartbeat

Constricts Bronchi

Stimulates Peristalsis & secretion

Stimulates Release of bile

Contracts Bladder

Sympathetic

Dilates Pupils

Inhibits flow of saliva

Accelerates Heartbeat

Dilates Bronchi

Inhibits Peristalsis & secretion

Conversion of Glycogen to Glucose

Secretion of Adrenaline & Noradrenaline

Inhibits Bladder Contraction

The Vagus nerve starts vibrating when there is activity in the Left Frontal Cortex. 'Healing' messages are sent to all the organs that everything is well. We relax and feel good. The inner organs start working at their optimum level.

> When our organs function at their optimum our immune system is being strengthened. We feel less pain as our bodies and our brains build up resilience.

The lungs will take in sufficient oxygen and get rid of the carbon dioxide waste, the heart will beat regularly and the digestive system will absorb the nutrition in our food and discard waste[5]. This is called the **para-sympathetic system;** it is activated by optimistic thoughts and by positive emotions. It is a healing and well-being cycle.

Well-being and Happiness become accessible even if we are stressed.

As we now know the amygdala tends to be stimulated even when there is no danger but the good news is that activity in the L-PFC (the management centre for positive emotions) allows signals to travel freely back and forth to the amygdala (see pages 16 and 17 for visual images). This helps us to assess whether there is an actual danger or not.

Our L-PFC can gauge that everything is okay, when for example the snake we thought we saw in front of us was actually just a little branch. The amygdala is then signalled to stop alerting our defence system. Instead the Vagus Nerve is activated helping us to relax and enjoy our lives. Stress does not built up and we remain healthy and well.

It sounds simple, and it is, as long as we remember to activate our left, rather than right, management system which literally creates our destiny.

Well-being ratio of 4 to 1[2]

There is one last discovery we need to remember before looking at what we can do to create this super-positive brain activity that will make such a change in our lives.

Research shows that we need a ratio of at least four positive thoughts to one negative thought to operate at our optimum and fully enjoy daily living.

You may have noticed how we tend to focus on the one critical remark in spite of getting ten encouraging remarks. This is our natural survival instinct.

We do not want to get hurt or to look foolish or be rejected by others.

To free ourselves from sensitivity to negative feed-back and information, we have to make a conscious effort to give more attention to the many positive messages that are sent our way. We need at least 4 times more positive than negative information circling around our brains in order to flourish and not fall under the spell of anxiety, worry or anger.

Gratitude multiplies Positive Feelings; it Changes The Brain

Professor Robert Emmons was one of the psychologists who was immediately invited onboard in 1998 when the focus in psychology changed to investigate what brings well-being and happiness. He already had discovered that the ancient qualities of gratitude and appreciation were extremely empowering especially for people who were feeling down or depressed.

It is amazing to realise that gratitude was highly regarded by the Roman author and politician Cicero who lived a century before Christ, as one of the quickest ways to well-being. Emmons[6] explains gratitude as a realisation that we have not got to where we are without much help from others. Gratitude is a realisation that we have good experiences. It is an appreciation of life and nature as gifts to be minded.

> Gratitude is an intense awareness that good things happen to us, an awareness that we meet good people.

Emmons and his team noticed that people who are grateful tend to be less materialistic, they compare themselves less with others, are less greedy, less angry and more likely to help others. These people cope better with stress and trauma.

Interestingly after the 9/11 twin tower disaster a large number of people used gratitude as a coping mechanism in order to recover from the loss of loved ones[7].

Survivors of 9/11
were grateful

- to still be alive
- for other loved ones to still be alive
- for the people who had been willing to risk their lives to save others

21

Gratitude has helped numerous people to recover from depression. It is now used as a prescription by a number of doctors due to its ability to empower people with physical and mental illness and to help them recover more quickly.

Gratitude is so powerful that many psychologists now believe that by the year 2050 it will be quite normal to take regular time out to do mental fitness exercises, such as gratitude writing and gratitude contemplation (see the brain train exercises further on) in order to stay mentally and physically healthy.

Gratitude in Action

Imelda is twenty years old and her mother is a heroin addict. Her father died from cancer and alcoholism. Her grandmother who was her anchor in life developed Alzheimer's Disease and died. Imelda now lives with her other grandmother who tends to be strict and critical but somehow Imelda is a really bubbly and happy person. She uses gratitude to keep herself well;

> *Often I wake up amazingly bright in the morning but when I go downstairs I would meet this cranky negative granny.*

One day I decided to write down all the things I appreciated about her and all that she does for me and I've seen great results from it. Once I started being grateful I saw the little things she was doing for me and I appreciated them more and now we are in a better relationship.

She tends to act like a strict mother so we don't do 'granny' things, I suggested for example that we go for lunch but there was always an argument so I decided to forget about that idea. Then out of the blue she invited me out for lunch. Afterwards she says 'we should do this more often'. I am delighted of course.

What I have realised is that I can't change her, I can only change how I look at her and where I put her in my life. I have decided to be grateful and suddenly she seems to have changed and I love it.

Gratitude stimulates the pleasure hormone dopamine and the mood enhancing hormone serotonin. These hormones also help to regulate sleep and improve our memory. Our brain activity becomes clearer[8]. With persistence a new brain pathway is created which is like a new habit of thinking differently. We are creating an increased awareness that good things happen to us, that we are surrounded by a lot of goodness and that we can increase good experiences in our lives. When it comes to the brain the principle of 'use it or lose it' very much applies[4].

Gratitude Apps

> There is a number of Gratitude Apps that can be downloaded on a mobile phone or tablet to help us keep up the practise of the following Gratitude Skills.

BRAIN TRAIN

To Be Grateful

Gratitude is not an excuse to ignore daily challenges and negative events but it can give us the strength to cope better. Gratitude can help us to choose our battles, to know where to put our energy. Gratitude works well in harmony with the other well-being skills described in this book, some which help to turn a negative situation into benefit.

Gratitude oils the mechanism of the brain and its positive emotional life.

The following skills can increase your happiness and well-being no bounds, once practised.

1. **Recall good events in your life**
2. **Keep a Gratitude Journal**
3. **Write a Gratitude Letter**
4. **Pause for Gratitude Contemplation**
5. **Say 'Thank You'**

1. Recall Good Events in Your Life

In my 6 week course, workshops and well-being getaways I always introduce the gratitude skill early on. Within thirty minutes I am sure to give participants an opportunity to recall something good in their lives. It can be something small or something big, it does not matter. What matters is that a person becomes aware that something good has happened to them recently.

In addition I would ask the participants to think about how they might have contributed to this experience. Sometimes that surprises people, but if for example I dwell on the beautiful sunrise I experienced this morning and how I might have contributed to that I might realise that 'yes' I did go out of my way, I went down by the sea-shore for a little walk rather than stay in bed.

The reflection on what we did to put ourselves in the way of good experiences makes us aware of the power we have to direct ourselves towards many uplifting experiences.

BRAIN TRAIN

The Appreciation formula:

1.

Write down or think about something good that happened to you lately ....

....

....

....

2.

Write down or think about how you helped to make that happen? ....

....

....

....

Example:

Something good.. *My brother in Denmark sent me a lovely message on his birthday that he would have loved me to be there celebrating with him.*

I helped make that happen by: *sending him a text congratulating him and telling him how fortunate I feel to have him as my brother.*

If one wishes to take this further one might answer the following:

3.   Why this event is important to me:

....

....

....

Example:

This is important to me because... *I did not see my brother for 16 years as I lived very far away and could not get back home. Still he and his children were the first to collect me at the airport in the middle of a snowstorm the day when I did eventually get to go home. Also, whenever I go home I know he will welcome me and want me to spend time with him and the family.*

Sharing the experience

In my workshops I would ask people to share their gratitude reflection with the person next to them. Without fail the atmosphere is suddenly buzzing with chat and laughter.

With a small group I usually invite people to share with the group as this is a very uplifting way of getting to know one another. It also reinforces the idea that good things are happening to all of us - once we open our eyes.

It takes courage to share because we might reveal something personal and meaningful to another but it is as if gratitude is multiplied when everyone shares their story of good fortune. Good things are happening all around even if one or two people choose not to share just then.

In some families at dinner time each person shares the highlight of the day, and sometimes the low point of the day. Sharing the highlights brings everyone closer and more capable of accepting the unavoidable low points of the day. Solutions are more likely to be found in the spirit of optimism.

WWW

In some schools where they are now teaching positive

psychology life-skills, the teacher starts off the day by writing WWW on the blackboard. The pupils are then asked to share 'What Went Well?' either with the class, in groups or with their neighbour.

WWW

What went well since last we met? ....

....

....

....

This is the story of Stephen, an accomplished musician and his wife Dee:

Dee has a very stressful management job. She would come home and offload all the difficulties she has experienced through the day onto Stephen who would patiently listen but feel incapable of helping.

After taking a class in Gratitude skills Stephen decided to initiate the after-work conversation with Dee by asking her whether something good had happened at work that day. Dee was delighted to report on various events that had gone really well and how she felt she had made a difference. They both felt really uplifted and happy.

Suddenly Dee was able to get a more objective perspective on the difficulties she experienced, which after all were far outweighed by the positive experiences she had.

Three Good Things Once a Week

With adolescents who might be more cautious about sharing out loud, it has been very useful for them instead to write down 'Three good things' that happened to them lately.

It may seem like a drop in the ocean to only write down something good once a week but it is amazing how it starts a whole new thought process making us aware that actually quite a number of good things happen to us.

Three good things that have happened to me lately:

1..
....
....

2..
....
....

3..

....

....

....

A Gratitude Tree or Box

Some schools have a gratitude tree or a gratitude box in the lobby or in the classroom where one is encouraged to write anonymous little notes about good things that have happened. The principal or teacher might at some point organise an assembly where these notes are read out. This highlights the value of noticing the many good events and people in our lives.

We should not ignore problems or run away from dealing with negative events but even in business it is now recognised that those who focus on what goes well have greater success and find ways to continually reinvent themselves.

> In business it is now recognised that those who start a meeting focusing on what went well before looking at problems have a much better chance of finding helpful solutions.

2. Keep A Gratitude Journal

Keeping a regular journal of appreciation for everything that we experience as blessings in our lives is similar to WWW, but broader, as it may include looking deeper into the many ordinary privileges that we experience in our daily living. We might become more aware of

- where our food comes from
- the enjoyment of work
- leisure activities
- family life
- nature
- music etc, etc.

It is very personal how often one wishes to write in the journal of appreciation. A number of people find it more beneficial to write once a week rather than every day, which might make it too much of a chore. To keep up the habit we need to experience the satisfying elements of doing it[9 & 10].

Gillian, a care-worker and mother of four, has been struggling to keep herself well and happy for a number of years as she grew up thinking she was never good enough. Gratitude is one of the life-enhancing skills that she uses to create a beautiful life for herself:

When something inside me keeps telling me that I am not good enough I find it helpful to use the affirmation: 'I focus on my many blessings'.

I would write down my feelings first thing in the morning, then make a gratitude list and a list of what I want to attract over the day. This helps me to ease into the day on a positive note.

Advanced Journaling

Gratitude for things that go against us is an advanced well-being skill that can help us to accept adversity and make the best of it.

In Sport

Carl Lewis the multiple Olympic Gold medal winner used gratitude journaling as part of his daily exercise routine to turn his frustration with his competitors into gratitude for them.
Lewis chose to be grateful for the opponents who continually challenged him to do so much better as an athlete because they were so brilliant. He was forced to perform even better.

3. Write A Gratitude Letter[11]

One of the most successful gratitude practices that Positive Psychology has found conducive to a considerable increase in happiness and well-being is writing a gratitude letter to a person who has made a hugely positive impact on one's life.

Imelda found great benefit from writing such a letter:

At one point I wrote a gratitude letter to my nanny and my dad who have both passed away. It was all about what I missed about them. I got so emotional, it wasn't sad emotions, it was all the good memories that I had, and I wished I had thought of writing this before. I started bawling because I remembered my dad's bad jokes, my nanny's ice-cold hands and her minding me and I am so glad to have these memories.

Writing a gratitude letter to someone who has been good to us or who has inspired us gives us an opportunity to focus intensely on how someone else went out of their way to support us at a particular time in our lives.

Reading this letter out or handing it to the other person can have additional benefits as we are giving someone an insight into a goodness that we have received from them which has made a lasting impression.

In Schools

In some schools children or young people are asked to write a gratitude letter to their parents and give it to them. Also, the parents are asked to write a letter to their child/teenager telling them what they appreciate about them.

> *In the classroom pupils can also be asked to write a gratitude letter to someone who they do not necessarily get to meet but who has inspired them in some way or another. It can be to Nelson Mandela, a grandfather who has died or even a dog who has been a faithful friend.*

4. Pause for Gratitude Contemplation[12]

Gratitude contemplation means to write down or think about something or somebody one is grateful for and then, to simply sit and hold on to that memory and feeling for a while. It is sometimes called Savouring or Mindfulness. Holding a feeling of gratitude for a while is a simple way to increase positive emotions.

> By holding on to a positive memory for 30 seconds we allow it to establish itself as a long-term memory in the hypocampus which is our memory store.

When we repeatedly dwell on good experiences, little by little we build up a nice store of positive experiences which we then can draw on when we experience problems and meet adversities. This enables us to access an optimistic outlook which might otherwise escape us when we are overcome by adverse circumstances.

BRAIN TRAIN

Gratitude contemplation :

1. Simply be still while noticing your own breathing for 30 seconds allowing yourself to APPRECIATE BEING ALIVE. Do this a few times over the day.

or

2. Allow yourself to focus on some good event or something you like in your environment and simply, **Sit with that experience for 30 seconds.**

Pausing several times a day whilst focusing on a good event is extremely conducive to creating many new positive pathways in the brain. **This deliberately chosen gratitude pause increases serotonin and dopamine activities which activate our immune system.**

> We can experience a wonderful mood lift and build up stamina to deal with life's challenges in the most beneficial manner.

5. Say 'Thank You'

The neuroscientist Richard Davidson recommends to simply looking someone in the eye and say thank you as a way of creating positive emotional brain activity. This connects us to other people in an uplifting and bonding manner. It signals to the brain and immune system that all is well and that the world is a good place.

His research shows that when a person is being thanked they automatically feel like passing on that sentiment to others around them. It is like a chain reaction of positive emotions. It is simple and it works.

BRAIN TRAIN

Saying 'Thank You':

Look out for opportunities to thank people. Look the person in the eye and if appropriate shake their hand or hug them and say 'thank you' for something you appreciate.

The Gratitude Dance

For fun Matt decided to do a crazy little Gratitude Dance in a public place and asked his girl-friend to film it. They uploading it on You Tube and got a lot of hits.

Then somebody funded them to travel to as many countries as possible to perform and film this short, crazy little dance. In this You Tube clip you can see how people joined him in the Gratitude Dance wherever he went.

www.youtube.com/watch?v=Ri9PpFVyVhE

Treat Yourself to a Gratitude Dance

First thing in the morning, in private if you like, do a little gratitude dance. You might be surprised at how powerful this is.

When I was growing up I loved it when I was alone in the house. I put on music in the sitingroom and danced around. I still enjoy it – when I remember to do it.

CHAPTER TWO

SELF-KINDNESS, SELF-MINDING

Without Self-kindness and Self-compassion we will never be able to accept our own and other peoples short-comings. Self-kindness is crucial to our well-being and ability to create those nourishing micro-moments of connection with other people.

Self-minding
or Self-pampering?

Self-kindness might sound as if we are letting ourselves off the hook and not taking responsibility for anyone but ourselves. We are looking out for Number One and making ourselves the centre of our world. However, research shows that people who are mentally troubled often are overly harsh on themselves.

Often people who are mentally ill have had an experience which has wounded them and robbed them of self-respect and self-confidence. Salt is rubbed into the wound by self-criticism and expecting more from oneself than is humanly possibly considering these past hurtful experiences. Wounds need special care, gentleness and rest.

Self-kindness facilitates healing, it frees up energy and creativity and enables us to contribute something worthwhile.

Most of us carry unintended wounds inflicted by someone close to us who might themselves have been wounded.

Self-kindness helps us to view ourselves with compassion so that we do not push ourselves beyond reason. It prevents burn-

42

out and illness because we are working with who we really are rather than who we wish to be. To self-mind is honest and nourishing to ourselves and others.

Self-compassion

Kristen Neff is a Professor of Self-compassion, she discovered the necessity of self-kindness when she realised that her 8-year old son had Autism. She blamed herself for not knowing how to cope and for not having realised sooner that this was his condition. Self-compassion as she calls it enabled her to forgive herself. It reminded her that she was doing the best she knew how to and to take time out to mind herself.

'The Horseboy' is a documentary about Kristin and her husband going on an adventure to bring their son to a Mongolian Shaman for healing. The family-bond is strengthened and they all discover a lovely new development in their son who befriends another boy and the shaman.

Kristin explains the three elements of self-compassion:

- **Self-kindness**
- **Seeing oneself as part of the human family**
- **Taking time out to be quiet and connect with one's deeper self**

43

People using self-compassion skills have been found to be incredibly well and happy in their lives[1]. In my own research I discovered that many people were not particularly happy in their lives, but those who were, all had higher levels of self-compassion.

Self-Criticism versus Self-Kindness

Self-criticism which is the opposite of self-kindness has been linked with negative childhood experiences such as not being soothed or consoled in moments of distress and being neglected or penalised rather than helped to accept weakness and failure as an unavoidable characteristic of being human. In most cases this lack of love in our childhood did not happen because our parents or carers were mean, it happened because nobody is perfect. Everyone, including our parents or carers is human and has moments of weakness and failings.

Even with an abundance of good childhood experiences we might unawares pick up anxiety and judgement as ways of pushing us to do better. This happened to Aoife who has two loving parents. She entered 4th year in school and suddenly felt overwhelmed by pressure to pass final exams even though the exams were 2½ years away. The pressures were so strong that she started self-harming to get rid of it.

44

This is her story of how she had to learn to be self-kind:

Medication did not solve my problems but it enabled me to calm down and face my problems and discover what I needed to do. I had to learn to organise my thoughts and tell myself that doing the Leaving Cert wasn't that bad. These exams may be the worst exams I would ever have to tackle but once it was over I would be able to relax.

When I had a problem with science I found taking a couple of hours doing arts or something I enjoyed enabled me to approach science differently. I would then simply give it a certain amount of time, it was a job that needed to be done, I did it and then I could forget about it. It was no longer so big in my life.

Self-judgement and self-criticism can undermine us as they activate our threat system making us feel inadequate. We feel incompetent or not good enough, we become afraid of not measuring up. Also, our consumer society bombards us with images of perfection and success urging us to look better and perform unceasingly.

Fear creates an over-production of cortisol hormones which over time build up as a toxin in our bodies[3].

45

Society is competitive. We can feel we need to be better than average which makes life very difficult because average keeps changing. It is like sales people who are expected to keep selling more; every month the target goes up making impossible demands on time and energy. Once we do better everyone else might also do better so we are still average[4].

In Japan young workers are dying from exhaustion because the job is always on their mind making it impossible to relax. Young people who are gifted in other areas than what our educational system offers or what is highlighted in the media, may feel ignored and worthless unless they learn how to be self-kind.

Of course we need to strive to improve ourselves and do better but this will happen naturally without us pushing ourselves when we learn to put our health and well-being first, when we learn to do more of what we love doing.

Being self-kind helps people to experience less anxiety and depression. Self-kindness cultivates a tolerant and a non-judgemental attitude towards oneself. A lack of self-kindness brings discouragement and intolerance often followed by mental difficulties and stress related brain-activity[2] (for visual images of the stress and relax systems see page 17).

High Self-Esteem
versus Self-Kindness

One would think that having a high self-esteem would be to our advantage, at a closer look however high self-esteem tends to lead to narcissism which is an exaggerated preoccupation with oneself. While a number of psychologists have recommended that one increases self-esteem as an anti-dote to low self-esteem, it has turned out that encouraging high self-esteem often makes people self-absorbed and even dishonest.

High self-esteem can be built on viewing oneself as better than others in a particular area but when one then experiences failure in that area one might lie and pretend that one didn't fail in order to hold on to that self-esteem.

This explains how someone takes his own life when he publicly fails at something; it is as if his whole world collapses because his self value is based on a specific skill, and not on who he is.

Sometimes we can fall into total despair thinking that all is lost when something happens that destroys our self-image of being competent in a particular area. But we are so much more than what we are good at.

47

Self-kindness
allows us to learn

Striving for high self-esteem tends to brush aside negative feedback and trivialise failure. Self-kindness on the other hand allows a person to face a failure and say 'okay, that didn't work out so well. I wonder what do I need to do differently?'. 'Do I need to apologise and make amends?' 'How do I move on and learn from this?'

Hannah had some rough years during her teens. When she was 16 she moved away from home to help a boyfriend with mental health problems. She always wore black clothes and black facial make-up; she dropped out of school and refused to discuss any of this with her parents and counsellors. Fortunately, her parents' increased tolerance and Youth Service's consistent offer of support helped her to move beyond wanting to self-harm to being an amazing bright and sociable person who is now studying child psychology. This is her story of how she learned to keep herself well and happy:

I went through a period in my life when everything was wrong. Hormones. Puberty.... I became aware that I was cranky all the time. That did not get me anywhere. I realised I had to choose my battles instead of being moody and difficult about everything. Sometimes it is important to react but other times I realised that it was not worth it.

While it is important to be considerate to other people one's own happiness is also important. If I start getting angry or irritated about something, it is better that I sleep on it or do something completely different otherwise the situation becomes ten times more negative.

When I sleep on something the whole thing becomes positive because I view it from a different angle. Doing something different doesn't work as well because I might start thinking about it again and get upset while I can easily fall asleep and wake up with a different point of view. I don't know anyone else who operates like that, most of my friends would panic and not be able to sleep but this is the way I get re-charged and then I am so happy when I wake up. I think about my problem or situation not because I have to, but because I want to. That's my solution.

The studies I do now are much better because it is long-distance learning. I can do it at a time that suits me; it doesn't matter when I do it as long as I hand in assignments at the right time. It is just so much easier for me to learn when I don't have to force myself to get up early but can work at my own bio-rhythm.

It took a while for my family to accept this is how I am. My other two siblings are not like this and my parents didn't like that I was different. But that is ok, I do what I do and they do what they do. It has helped them view people and things from another angle.

To Live according to our Full Potential for Goodness

Self-kindness is a skill we can develop which enables us to know and accept ourselves and live according to our full potential for goodness.

As long as we push ourselves or judge ourselves harshly we are hurting rather than helping ourselves which makes it difficult for us to help anyone else.

It may not be easy to change from being self-critical and self-judging when we feel we do not measure up to our own, or to other people's expectations.

We might have an in-built defence system which has helped us survive by putting ourselves down, we may even feel comfortable thinking we are no good.

50

Marianne Williamson's famous statement which Nelson Mandela used in his inaugural speech when he became the President of South Africa expresses it well:

> "It is our light, not our darkness that
> most frightens us. We ask ourselves,
> 'Who am I to be brilliant, gorgeous,
> talented and fabulous?'
> Actually, who are you not to be?[6]"

We might not want to be aware of our own talents and gifts for fear of being put down when we start using them. We might not want to make 'a show' of ourselves and yet we may secretly dream of success and fulfilment. **Why are we afraid?**

Perhaps we do not get enough encouragement to follow our own unique interests and talents. Someone may put pressure on us to compete when we would rather do something for the enjoyment and social connection aspect. Someone may have given us a role that they want us to fulfil so that they feel safe but without considering whether this helps our well-being.

Self-kindness is paying attention to our needs and interests - giving time to develop and enjoy these.

Successful people are not necessarily those who finished school but rather those who used their passion and talents in the service of others. They took the risk of being laughed at for being different. Marshall Rosenberg[5] who is known for his work on non-violent communication advocates our special need to contribute to the well-being of others as one of our most fundamental needs. However, there may be personal blockages that inhibit our ability to contribute to the well-being of others. Self-kindness can help loosen these blockages.

We Can Rewire Our Brains

Self-kindness can be developed through positive, soothing self-talk as this creates intensely positive activity in the left front brain area which is connected to millions of brain-neurons. This positive self-soothing talk is not something we invent, it is tuning in to something deeper within ourselves.

My Story:

Self-kindness is something I have to work on continually as

I have an overly developed ability to view myself from someone else's most negative perspective.

When I say something and do not see a smile, hear words of approval or at least see some sign of interest in what I say or do I automatically think I am doing something wrong or unimportant. I start doubting my own motives and head towards despair. But I am learning to ask myself 'What are you doing?' and when I think about it my honest answer is 'I'm putting myself down'.

I then change my question and ask: 'What is your intention? What do you want?' This connects me to my deep desire to bring well-being skills into the educational system. A desire to prevent depression, anxiety and suicides by offering well-being skills to young people from an early age onwards. I do not know whether I will succeed but I know if I do not try, I will have ignored who I am and what I want.

Untold positive activities take place in the brain when we 'feed' it with up-lifting, soothing and caring activities and information. We physically rewire our brains through habits of self-kindness; these raise our mood and increase our optimism, altruism, self-confidence, focus and memory[7].

53

By being self-kind we are building a bank of positivity within, that helps us to deal with humiliations and sufferings in a constructive and dignified manner.

By not continually going over and over past events and opportunities that we lost out on (ruminating) but rather taking in the gift of the present moment, and noticing the goodness around us we are rewiring our brain to work to the optimum for our well-being.

BRAIN TRAIN

To Become Self-Kind

1. Write a Self-encouragement letter
2. Pinpoint when you are at your best
3. State what you love through the bubble schema
4. Self-hug
5. Take a breath

1. Write a Letter of Self-Encouragement

By looking at ourselves as a best friend we will know how to encourage ourselves regarding the person we are, our interests, our good intentions and our future hopes. When no one else is around to encourage or understand us we can support ourselves by writing a self-encouraging letter:

Dear .... (your name) *I am very fond of you because* ....
....
and...
....

It is great to know you as I see you as a person who...........................
....

You are a unique person who..
....

I wish you every success in ....
.... ,

By writing an encouraging letter to ourselves we are helping our brains to interpret our lives with hope and courage. We are gaining access to our deeper and more genuine self which lies behind the opinions of others and the pressures of the surrounding world to conform to their idea of success.

Writing a self-encouraging letter is an opportunity to get to know ourselves and our deepest aspirations and desires. It is an opportunity to wish ourselves well and to regain an innocent view of ourselves. If we do not know our best selves how can we put it forward? If we do not know our deepest aspirations, how can we strive to fulfil them?

Optional Extra:

Read out loud your letter in the company of a trusted friend, family or in an intimate group setting. Reading out your personal self-encouragement is an act of courage because you reveal who you really are. The advantage is that it may help others to understand and support you better, and give them the courage to be self-kind.

Self-encouragement in our work place

By writing a letter of support to ourselves regarding the work we do, the efforts we put in and the co-operation we give to others we are clarifying our contribution to society. We also give ourselves an opportunity to re-assess how meaningful our work is to us personally and to review whether this is the best place to be at this point of our life.

> We may be in a job that makes us feel safe and that might be enough - but sometimes we need to put ourselves forward for something that is more meaningful.

Self-kindness is to look at all our needs ensuring that we are doing our best to live the life we want to live rather than the life that others expect us to live.

It is important to know how to supply ourselves with the kindness that others may fail to show us. This way when other people are busy or in bad form we can still be encouraged and create a safe place within ourselves. When others do not recognise our good qualities we can recognise them for ourselves; we can care for ourselves. We can 'self-parent'.

Self-encouragement
in the classroom

When children and young people get this opportunity to self-encourage it is an invitation to become more independent of other people's behaviour.

Writing the letter of self-encouragement can help us not to get stressed or discouraged by negative influences in our environment.

Recording and
Listening to Comforting Statements

It can be fun for example to use a mobile phone to record some self-comforting messages which we can then listen to last thing at night or first thing in the morning.

My Example:

'Michaela, you are doing really well. I love the way you're so dedicated to transmitting Positive Psychology Life-Skills to as many individuals you possibly can. You spend time every day improving and preparing a book which will be helpful to many. Your book will be encouraging and helpful to people across all walks of life because what you write about is relevant to all of us: the art of cultivating happiness and well-being at a deep and life-giving level. ... etc'

These whispers of encouragement can express our deepest motivations and thoughts. The more we listen to and identify with these the more our better and deeper self will surface and give us the courage to be who we really are.

2. Pinpoint When You Are At Your Best

Recall your best experiences in order to increase them.

Taking time to write down or talk about when we function at our best honours a genuine part of ourselves which needs to be nourished. This process is used to help improve the atmosphere and well-being in work places. Appreciative Inquiry[8] (AI) as it is called consists of reflecting on and expressing what is one's best experience of work, and then making a plan of how to create opportunities to repeat this.

> By deliberately dwelling on what we do when we function at our best, we might find ways to increase these activities.

Seeking out the situations where we are at our best can lift us out of a negative mind frame that makes life miserable.

Rather than allowing ourselves to be victimised by a negative situation we can start pursuing enjoyable activities.

When we are in a positive mood we become more creative, open-minded and productive in every area of our lives. What seemed like a huge problem suddenly becomes an interesting challenge.

BRAIN TRAIN

Discover
You at Your Best

Reflect on and continue the following statement/s:

I love my life when I...
....
....
....

I am at my best at work when ....
....
....
....

I am at my best in my relationships or friendships when I...
....
....

....

....

I am at my best in my leisure time when I..............................

....

....

....

I am at my best spiritually when I.......................................

....

....

....

**These affirmations can also be used in conversations
between friends, family or in a trusted group setting.**

Creative activity that I love doing:…......
....
....

I will think of myself as
…..................
....

People I love spending time with:................
…....................
....

Physical activity that I love:.................
....
....

MY SELF-KINDNESS HABITS

Charities I want to assist:
....
....
.....

Nourishing Foods I love
....
....
....

Music I love:
....
....
....

Places I love going to:
…...................
....
....

Groups I would love to join: ....
…....................
....

Books/films I will enjoy:
…....................
....
....

Ways I enjoy being spiritual
…......…..........
....
....

BRAIN TRAIN

3. Establish what you love doing through the Self-Kindness Bubbles diagram

The Self-Kindness Bubbles diagram opposite is another opportunity to anchor more deeply in our consciousness what it is we care about and want to be involved with. The more clearly we focus on something the more opportunities we will suddenly notice in our surroundings to engage in these activities.

The Self-Kindness Bubbles can be used individually, with a friend or in a group/class setting. When a person has filled in the bubbles they can take turns sharing their answers with each other.

> When we listen to each other's stories we expand our own understanding of self-kindness and get ideas on how to mind ourselves better.

APP for Scheduling Positive Events

The US Army has created a free APP called POSITVE ACTIVITY JACKPOT where you can click to spin the slot-machine which then stops on an activity that you might find enjoyable. Before you spin the wheel you can choose a particular category such as indoor, water activity, restaurant/food, physical activity, shopping, travel etc.

You can keep trying your luck until you find an activity that suits or you can turn on the GPS function to help you locate something in your area. The APP can be downloaded from Google Play. This is their explanation:

Pleasant Event Scheduling

Positive Activity Jackpot uses a professional behavioural health therapy called pleasant event scheduling (PES), which is used to overcome depression and build resilience. This app features augmented reality technology to help users find nearby enjoyable activities and makes activity suggestions with local options and the ability to invite friends. If you cannot make up your mind which fun thing to do, "pull the lever" and let the app's jackpot function make the choice for you.

4. Self-Hug
(do you dare?)

To hug oneself might sound weird but it actually can bring a great boost to well-being.

This caring embrace builds up our immune system and helps us to feel good about ourselves. For some it can be a spiritual experience as they connect to something beautiful within. Some people might imagine a loving Creator being part of that hug possibly whispering 'I love you...' 'You are my beautiful creation.' 'I

> Hugging oneself releases oxytocin, a hormone in the brain which gives us a feeling of closeness, safety and wellness.

have lots of wonderful gifts in store for you.' etc.

We might take the opportunity to also give or ask for a hug from a trusted friend or family member as this opens our awareness of the goodness and kindnesses we are surrounded by in our lives. It also builds up confidence to pursue activities and positive thinking patterns that we might not access when we feel uninspired and unlovable.

5. Take A Breath

This is a particular meditation or mindfulness experience that many people find calming and empowering:

Sit quietly while you tune in to your breath.

Now allow yourself in your mind to walk to a safe beautiful place whether it is a beach, a church, a park or a forest clearing. Here you stop and rest for a while enjoying its peaceful surroundings. You might imagine yourself sitting or lying down taking it all in. The sounds, the smells, the visual beauty and the feeling of the sand or grass beneath you.

After a while imagine yourself walking back to where you started.

A sample of this type of guided meditation can be found on

the website www.HappinessSkills.ie. It can be downloaded and enjoyed as an individual, with a friend or in a group.

OTHER RESOURCES

Other **Self-Minding Reflections and Meditations** can be found on the You Tube channel **'The Honest Guys'**. These visually beautiful and auditorily comforting videos are created by Sian, Rick and Kev who freely offer these as a help to meditation and relaxation. They discovered the power of time out to recover from stress and anxiety and connect to a deeper peace within.

Listen to and download from:

http://thehonestguys.co.uk/

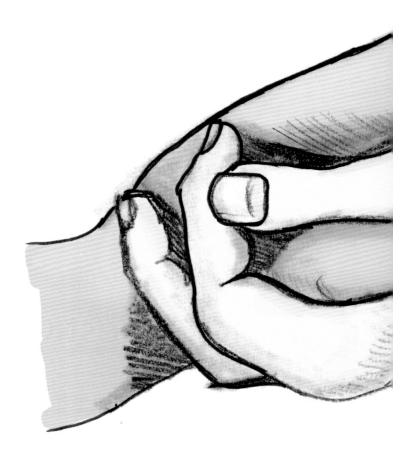

CHAPTER THREE

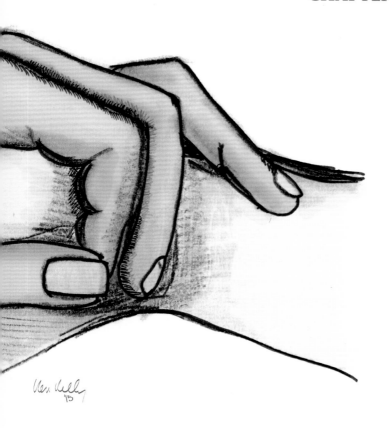

POSTIVE RELATIONSHIPS

Positive Relationships make us feel safe and trusted. With the support of one another we can make hugely positive changes in the lives of those around us. But how do we keep our relationships positive?

Positive Relationship

Our greatest strength is other human beings[1]. From early on in life we thrive through closeness to at least one other person. When we are tiny infants closeness is experienced from one or two adults. 'The 'Rescuing Hug' true story illustrates that a caring connection to a sibling can also make all the difference:

This incident took place in Philadelphia Hospital when twins were born prematurely and one of them was dying in her incubator. Her twin sister on the other hand was thriving[2]. Nothing worked to make the dying twin better. A clever nurse, in spite of hospital warnings of cross-infection and threats of being sued for malpractice, decided as a last resort to put the dying twin into the incubator with her stronger sister.

Immediately the stronger twin put her arm around her weaker sister. Within minutes the weaker sister's heartbeat became normal. Within days she recovered and they both are healthy and strong today.

Medical practice has since changed and twins are now kept together after birth even if one of them is unwell. The positive connection that twins have created in the womb is now viewed as an asset to their well-being.

Our trust in others is determined by our early childhood experiences

Early childhood experiences greatly influence how much trust we have in people later on in life. The safer we felt in our childhood the more adventurous we could be because we knew that if something went wrong we could run right back to someone trusted[3]. We reached out and made positive connections with people around us.

Ideally we should all have experienced an abundance of positive communication early on in life but sometimes that did not happen due to our parents' or caregivers' illnesses or all-absorbing life-challenges. Also, some of us may have experienced traumatic abuse that destroyed or overshadowed the good connections which were there.

Many of us are wounded in certain areas of our emotional life. Some are deeply wounded by the lack of love connections. However it is never too late to heal and connect.

> We can learn to build positive relationships which can nourish and compensate for our initial lack of love[4].

The Positive Connection
of Friendship

Friendship is one of the most positive relationships a person can experience. A caring friendship connection gives us a positive self-image, a passion for life and the courage to care for people around us.

Strong positive connections build up a store of positive memories that helps us to feel at 'home' within ourselves. We feel supported and nourished and we grow in the awareness of having a positive influence in someone else's life[5].

Having this 'safe haven' in somebody who accepts us for who we are, someone who wants to listen to us and help us through difficulties is a great gift:

18 year old Ann-Marie feels extremely stressed due to exam pressure. She is also worried about what to do after the exams, but her positive relationships help her to cope:

> For the moment I go out a lot at the weekend and have fun and I don't really mind myself that well - I should really be at home doing the assignment that is stressing me out but it is as if I need breathing space. It is wonderful to be out with

friends. It is my friends whom I go to if I have problems and they in turn come to me. We mind each other. I have a core of five solid good friends with whom I can share everything.

I talk to friends but also to my mum and dad, they have so much more life experience than I have, they might have been through something similar and are able to view it from a different angle. Also my parents are so different from each other that I get a good variety of inputs. I then mull it all over and decide how to handle it. I might get inspiration from what they say and decide that perhaps my idea was a bit daft and needs to be adjusted - ever so slightly 😊

Incidentally, Ann-Marie did really well at her exams.

Activating
our Social Brain

A small part of the brain is dedicated to social IQ. Activity in the Fusiform Gyrus is all deciding regarding our social skills (see next page for a visual image). This little centre helps us to discern what is going on with other people.

Lack of activity in the Fusiform Gyrus can get us into some very awkward situations.

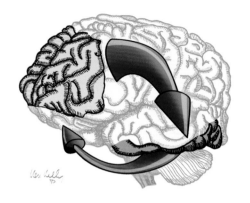

The Fusiform Gyrus (purple brain area) helps us to be sensitive to other peoples feelings. It helps us to know when to modify our behaviour, for example not to start dancing on the table or throw food around just because we feel like it. We sense when other people might not appreciate something just because we do. People with autism have less activity in this centre but it can be stimulated with special care.

When two open-minded people communicate with each other seemingly the Fusiform in both people starts vibrating with a similar energy, tuning into each other beyond verbal language and understanding. The more interested two people are in each other the greater the activity in this area.

The Amygdala (see chapters one and two) is very quick to signal alert/stand-by to all our organs, but this can be reversed when we create caring connections with people around us.

Positive relationships make us feel safe which affects our brains in a way that 'social' messages from the Fusiform

Gyrus can flow freely back and forth to the management centre at the front of our brains (see image opposite).

The Fusiform Gyrus informs us of how people are feeling and what they might expect. It helps us to tune in to what is needed in order to create a positive connection with somebody.

> When we are upset or stressed it is difficult for information to travel freely to the management centre which helps us to make wise decisions.

People with good social skills have a lot of activity in their Fusiform Gyrus. They might have had good role models as we tend to model ourselves on people near us. Or they might have made a personal decision to develop an awareness of their own and other people's feelings in order to know how best to connect with them.

Overly concerned about other people's feelings?

Funnily enough too much consideration of Fusiform Gyrus messages can become inhibiting and depressing. We can become so aware of other people's feelings and needs that we forget to listen to our own.

A person with an over-developed Fusiform Gyrus (like me) needs to learn to be more self-aware and assertive so as not to allow other people's needs to take up so much attention that one's energy and personality become non-existent.

> Self-awareness and assertiveness are imperative skills for the person who is overly concerned about other people's opinions and needs.

Good friendship can be a great help to learn to set boundaries within this safe environment. There is a balance of give and take. In friendship we develop social skills and automatically improve these as we interact with one another.

Building a store of Positive Connections

Sometimes due to past negative experiences which we have not fully processed we expect something bad to happen again even though we find ourselves in a completely different situation. However when we build a memory bank of positive connections with trusted people around us a brain pathway is created that enables us to say:

'Okay, maybe someone will not like what I say, but that does not matter, lots of other people might find it helpful'

'Perhaps someone will laugh but that is their problem not mine'.

'Perhaps someone will put me down but at least I will know to go elsewhere with my ideas'.

'Maybe that person is not much of a friend anyhow, but that does not mean I cannot be friendly'.

Holding on to Relationships

John and Julie Gottman, a U.S. professor couple, have investigated the 'secret' of couples who stay together[8]. One of their methods is to invite couples to spend time in a cosy little flat which is equipped with cameras and microphones that record the couple's interaction. The couple would be asked to sort out some ordinary house chores and bills together over a couple of hours. They would soon forget the cameras as there was no one else around. Afterwards the Gottman's would analyse the recorded interaction of the couple to see if they could find a pattern.

The Gottman's followed a large number of couples for over forty years and they found that there were mainly three types of couples:

- **The passionate couple** who were very vocal and dramatic in their communication, for good and bad.
- **The independent couple** who tended to lead separate lives.
- **The dependant couple** who were rarely seen apart and seemed to do everything together.

Furthermore the Gottmans discovered that no matter which type of the three relationships, the couples who stayed together had one common denominator namely that:

> **IN LASTING RELATIONSHIPS**
> couples communicate with a
> Ratio of 5 : 1 of
> Positive to Negative Interactions

The passionate couple might have hurtful arguments but as long as the passionate loving was five times more frequent the relationship would flourish.

The independent couple might grow apart but as long as they kept up a positive communication that was five times stronger than their lack of unity, the couple would have a thriving and lasting relationship.

The dependent couple might tend to avoid conflict in order not to upset one another but perhaps suddenly explode, but as long as their confrontation was followed by five times more positive interaction their relationship would last.

This research was mostly done in the U.S. where divorce is quite acceptable when one falls out of love. In other parts of the world couples may stay together for social or economic reasons.

Caring
Relationships

130,000 people of various ages and from a number of countries were asked in a Gallup Survey what made them happy. Most participants gave two answers: 'learning something new' and 'having someone you can count on in your life'[7]. But what is it that enables us to count on somebody?

These are the positive communication skills professors Harvey and Omarzu[14] and many other researchers observed that people in caring friendships and relationships use :

1   **Sharing of good news**
2   **Looking up to one another**
3   **Supporting 'crazy dreams'**
4   **Sharing a common vision**
5   **Helping someone to fulfil their goals**
6   **Talking about personal concerns**
7   **Honesty**
8   **Having Fun**
9   **Physical contact**

1. Sharing of Good News
(responding constructively)

Even the best of friends or partners will experience negativity from each other due to stress, past negative experiences and human nature. But when they communicate more about the good experiences in their lives, past negative experiences fade into the background and negative memories start to heal.

When two people are happy for each other's good, positive experiences they both benefit. One of them will feel truly supported and appreciated while the other one will feel uplifted from supporting a friend in their good fortune - it is almost as good as experiencing it oneself. Or is it?

> Something as simple as being happy for the success or good experiences of one's friend or partner is more predictable of a lasting relationship than the sharing of bad events although that has its place.

What about feeling jealous and envious?

It is a common human reaction to feel jealous or envious when we see someone else succeed at something or get something that we would have liked for ourselves. This can be a humiliating feeling which makes us feel uncomfortable. Rather than admitting to our feelings we might either criticise the other person involved or start feeling sorry for ourselves. Being happy for someone else might not come easily but honestly facing our own negativity might be the most productive in the long run.

My story:

Personally I've struggled with feelings of envy and jealousy to the point of shaking and feeling sick but I have reached a stage where I welcome these feelings because it points out to me when I am not fully engaged in my own life.

This is an opportunity to ask myself what I really want and look at what I need to do to get it.

If for some reason what I want I cannot have, I ask myself what I then would want instead?
If I cannot answer this question at least I know that there is something missing in my life and that I need to be on the look-out for something.

Instead of jealousy being a negative experience it becomes a kick-start to engaging myself more deeply in my own life.

Four ways of responding
to a friend's enthusiasm[12]

Keeping in mind our tendency to self-centredness and negativity it is easy to identify with the four different ways that we might respond when somebody shares something good that has happened to them:

1   'Oh yes, that's great' (and not meaning it)
        passive encouragement

2   'Oh yes that reminds me of when I...'
        passive discouragement

3   'That could turn very bad....... '
        active discouragement

4   'I am delighted for you. Tell me more!'
        active encouragement

BRAIN TRAIN

**Create multiple positive connections
with people around you[13].**

Which of the above four responses describes your reaction?

For one day try to respond with active encouragement whenever someone tells you something they are excited about.

Take an interest in someone and ask them about what they love doing, listen actively by nodding, smiling and showing that you are interested.

BRAIN TRAIN+

In a group, classroom or youth club

In groups of 5 play this game five times rotating the roles to allow everyone to experience each of the roles (write each role on a piece of paper to pass on at each change of roles):

1. The person with good news who excitedly shares with the group (can be made up or real)

2. The person who encourages but with a tone of indifference

3. The person who advises against being so happy, pointing out what could go wrong

4. The person who starts talking about their own experience ignoring the news

5. The person who is interested, asks questions and congratulates

This is usually a fun experience but also educational as we might feel deflated by another person's lack of interest or negative attitude when we are sharing our 'good news'. Also we might not want to be a 'spoil sport' but it is good to take on the different roles as it will remind of us of how easy it is to fall into a disempowering response.

2. Looking up to one another

Choosing people near us who are better than ourselves helps us to develop positively as we tend to take on the qualities and moods of people close to us[9]. Consequently, we need to choose our company carefully.

> Sometimes we might hold on to a friend who really isn't a friend any longer as they may not respect us or make us feel good about ourselves.

Imelda who stays with her grandmother due to her mother's inability to deal with her heroin addiction explains:

My uncle due to my granddad (his dad) dying, was not in a good place. He became a heroin addict. My mum who was his younger sister left home to help him but she ended up an addict herself. She spent most of her time in the pub and when she came home she would beat me up. I asked myself what would happen if I stayed with my mum. I definitely would not be able to finish school.

I hope she gets better but she kept hurting me by what she said, she was never pleased with what I did. She rang me once when she was trying to commit suicide and I just can't handle that so when my phone broke I got a new number which she doesn't know.

My boyfriend recently told me that he is an alcoholic. I've given him an ultimatum, if he does not get a job and find a way to stop drinking within the month I will leave him. I have feelings for him and I love him but I am not going to let him drag me down. I left my mum to get away from this.

Thankfully Imelda is in a good place today, she works with young people who have impaired hearing and associated problems. She loves this work and is much appreciated by those who run the organisation. Imelda seems to have a special gift in this area, having had hearing problems herself.

Good friends create vitality and excitement about life and its challenges. Research indicates that viewing another person as an expert or as having qualities we admire and want to learn from is another sign of a positive friendship.

My story:

I mentioned earlier that I tend to want to please other people to the point of ignoring my own needs and feelings and running myself down. This is deeply ingrained – possibly inherited from my mum.

I am fortunate though to have a very close friend who is the opposite to me in that respect. He believes in what he does, and 'tough' if other people have a problem with that (of course that can go too far also). I admire that quality – it reminds me to be strong and not to obsess about getting other people's approval. Spending time with this person helps me to be more balanced in my approach to life.

3. Supporting 'crazy' dreams

Sometimes we under-estimate the power we have to fuel or quench someone's dream. When couples grow apart they have stopped listening to each other's dream or sense of purpose in life.

What can bring a couple close again is the skill of sitting down and listening to each other's dream no matter how crazy or far fetched. Dreams are what get us up in the morning. Dreams give meaning to our lives. So unless we believe someone's dream will hurt others, we can make all the difference in someone's life by taking their dream seriously.

We do not need to have the same dream or vision for the future, although it can be wonderful if we do. Indeed we might share one part of our dream with one person and another part of our dream with another. The positive connection is the listening, the believing and the emotional support that we can give - that is what makes the difference.

BRAIN TRAIN

Listen to and
Share in other people's dreams
Once a week ask someone about their dream or goals in life.

Watch 'Invictus', 'Mandella, A Long Walk to Freedom', 'The Vow' or any other film based on a true story that shows how a person has a dream and eventually fulfils it through their commitment to hold on to that dream.

Read biographies of people who fulfilled their dreams like for example Christina Noble, Gandhi, Mother Teresa.

My dream:

My dream is to somehow make positive psychology life-skills available to as many people as possible as I believe this will minimise or prevent depression, suicides and many other problems that lead to unhappiness.

Some people might think I am crazy to think positive psychology skills can make that much of a difference but I believe the evidence is there – that the more information people get the more of a chance people have of establishing the well-being habits that are so conducive to happiness and optimism.

Friends who support me in following my dream enable me to keep writing and 'dreaming' in spite of slow progress. Even if in the end I should fail in fulfilling my dream at least I will have spent my life passionately and inspired.

Some years ago I showed my mum some life-skills booklets I had produced. This was shortly before she died at the age of sixty-three from Parkinson's disease coupled with mental illness and cancer of the spine. She looked at the booklets and uttered the most supportive and meaningful words I can ever remember her saying: 'I believe in you!' This was after someone else had told me that there was nothing new in there!
Mum's comment was small and yet it created an ongoing supportive connection between us, that I still feel is there today.

A step further than listening to and encouraging someone's dream is to ask them whether they have a plan as to how to achieve it.

4. Sharing a common vision

Having a shared vision of core values that are important in life is another worthwhile positive connection to make. Having a shared vision of going somewhere or doing a project together lends to a closer relationship and more exchange of energy as the two people involved can keep that vision alive for one another. When we experience a crisis of identity or a feeling of loss a friend is one who reminds us of who we are and what we are about, thus helping us to stay on track.

My story:

Some years ago I made two life-skills DVDs that many Irish schools used in their Health & Personal Development classes. I had a vision for the DVDs but it was only when I was working on a film-set and 'accidentally' got talking to a colleague that we discovered that we both believed in giving young people an awareness of the many positive choices that they could make for themselves.

- *Our shared vision enabled us to co-produce two youth DVDs which are still being used in schools and youth clubs. I would not have managed to produce these without my co-producer who enabled me to pay the young people who participated. Also he lent credibility to the DVDs by sharing his experience of mistakes he had made as a teenager due to lack of life-skills education. Through a shared vision and passion for the project we were able to get other people on-board which enabled us to film and edit these DVDs.*

BRAIN TRAIN

In Awareness
of your Relationship Values

One way of gaining awareness of personal relationship values is to look at all the roles we have in life and reflect on which values are important in each role:

Fill in the value table opposite

- horizontally with the different roles you might have in life. Please add your own.
- vertically write down the various values that may be important to you. Please add your own.
- Then tick off the values that you want to develop in each role (as the example shows)

Roles I have: Values I hold:	Example: Friend	Son / Daughter	Worker / Student	Artist / Musician	Carer / Parent				
Fairness	√								
Honesty	√								
Kindness									
Humour	√								
Loyalty	√								
Listening	√								
Care									
Optimism	√								
Purpose									
Diligence									

5. Helping someone
to fulfil their goals

Friends also help one another to fulfil goals. Early in life a parent can be a friend regarding care and protection in order for us to feel safe enough to experiment and learn.

We can have a number of friends according to the various goals we have.

During school years teachers can play a significant supportive role in children's and young people's lives, especially when there is a lack of stability or encouragement in the home environment[6].

When a teacher models how to manage and control emotions[10] and takes a positive interest in supporting a pupil, even a brief encounter has been shown to interrupt problem behaviour and give that young person a sense of community and connection.

Support around our interests and talents reduces the doubts and loneliness that we might otherwise experience, it enables us to move forward confidently and constructively. Unfortunately, not all school environments facilitate this personal teacher-to-pupil connection.

If we have not become fully clear around our own goals we can gain a lot by helping others fulfil theirs.

BRAIN TRAIN

**Ask a few people that you trust
what goals they have, and how
they go about fulfilling them.**

If appropriate you might be inspired to help them out in some way or another. Just your interest in someone's goals can help them become clearer about where to put their focus and energy for those goals to be fulfilled. You might also find yourself inspired to clarify and share your own goals.

6. Talking about personal concerns

(compassion, empathy)

Friendship is a wonderful way of learning to empathise and have compassion for someone who is different from us. By learning to listen and trying to really understand what is going on with a friend we develop our capacity to empathise and be compassionate.

Empathy is a crucial quality for creating positive connections with other people who might have different ideas or values to ours.

We might not agree with someone's attitude but we can still respect them as a person and wish them well. Talking things through helps some people while others might need us to listen to them and accept them for who they are.

This is Linda's story of how she got through a difficult period in her life after her boyfriend ended the relationship:

My boyfriend and I finally split up a little over a month ago. Mum wasn't around that much but my friend Aoife represents the positive relationship I have with someone. I can tell her everything and I know she'll never tell anyone else. I don't know what I would have done without her these last two months.

BRAIN TRAIN

To Listen
**Ask someone how they are and
what is going on in their life.**

To Share

**Tell someone close to you
what is going on in your life right now**

These two skills can also be used in pairs, small groups or the classroom where each person takes a turn to for example share for 5 minutes and then listen for 5 minutes.

If necessary an agreement can be made to keep confidential what one shares.

7. Honesty

Honesty has firstly to do with knowing our own feelings, our needs and thoughts and secondly to do with not hiding these from others. Honesty is a fine balance between self-awareness and prioritising what is important in a relationship.

Being honest does not mean sharing all our secrets or private thoughts, we choose which are relevant and appropriate depending on who we are with.

BRAIN TRAIN

To be Honest:

Look at this amazing You Tube clip of Sean Stevenson who has faced enourmous challenges physically and mentally (he lives with the condition Osteogenesis Imperfecta)

https://www.youtube.com/watch?v=VaRO5-V1uK0

For further reflection answer the following:

What self-image does Sean Stevenson have?...............................

....

....

....

How is Sean honest even though he does not define himself as disabled?..

....

....

What is your positive honesty about yourself?...........................

....

....

8. Having Fun

With a friend with whom we feel accepted, and whom we admire and care for we feel free to be silly and laugh at things that might otherwise bring us down. This can be very healing, it can help us to get through hurts and disappointments. We share our negative experiences but in a humorous way which allows us to learn and move on.

> A friend is also someone we can have fun with because we do not have to watch every word we say or be perfect in our actions.

BRAIN TRAIN

Be Humorous

Watch a pet or a small child who enjoys playing and having fun (plenty on You Tube).

Take a few minutes every so often to view your situation from a humorous angle.

Do something harmless but fun with a friend – only you know what would be fun for you both.

9. The Power of Touch

The skin is one of the most sensitive organs of the body. Some people make the mistake of linking all touch with sex but what about a pat on the back or shoulder, hugging, linking or holding someone, an arm around the shoulder or a squeeze of the hand? These are all non-sexual but sensing ways of showing our care and approval of somebody.

> When someone we trust touches us it triggers the 'cuddle' hormone oxytocin which calms the amygdala and helps us to feel safe and good about life.

We might at times gently touch our own face, rub our neck or hair, or hold our arms around ourselves, all gestures that calm us down and reduce stress in our bodies.

Touching can be particularly valuable with elderly people and infants as they may not communicate much verbally. The touch communicates a connection beyond words; someone else notices us and connects.

Touch Research

Touch between people has been researched in a number of situations:

In a college where a teacher was helping students to take their own pulse there was a big difference between the students whom she touched and those she did not. In the study where she randomly, briefly touched the wrist of some of the students when helping them, students who were touched reported a more positive attitude towards her, interpreting her as more competent. The students, with whom she made that brief physical contact felt more motivated to participate and do well in class.

In a study of customers in a store, who on entering the shop were handed a catalogue whilst briefly being touched on the arm, the ones who were touched tended to buy more and taste more produce on offer.

Another study was of a young man at a bus stop asking for direction; he would briefly touch helpful persons on the arm when thanking them. When 'accidentically' some of his papers fell the persons who had been touched were much quicker and more likely to help him pick them up.

The research also showed that in some countries men were not comfortable being touched by men while in other countries like France and Italy there would be no difference whether one was touched by a male or female. Both would perceive it as encouraging.

Touching and Abuse

No doubt some feel anxious about the idea of physical contact as it may remind them of inappropriate behaviour and people stepping over the line. Touching has been abused and turned into sexual abuse by a great number of people and we are right to be clear about what is acceptable and what is not. It is hugely detrimental when someone we trust abuses the touch to gratify their own lustful desire.

> Physical touching can be quite personal; not everyone likes it so it is important to check with others that they are okay with how we make that physical connection.

A person can make us feel safe and good but then suddenly inappropriate sexual touching takes over and destroys all trust.

It is hugely important to never go along with touch that makes us feel uncomfortable. It is not within the scope of this book to elaborate further on intimate relationships, suffice it to say, that touch is a beautiful way of telling someone that we approve of them, and of stimulating their feel good hormones (oxytocin) and well-being.

Touch like every other communication can also be abused should it be forced on someone or used for one's own satisfaction rather than as a shared connection appreciated by both. It is a pity though when fear of abuse stops these beautiful positive connections that are re-affirmed through friendly touches[9].

Check your motives

We would need to check our motives, of course, that we are touching someone for their benefit and not only because we like touching them. This is where verbal communication is important in that we ask each other, whether the touch we give or have given is okay, and whether it communicates something uplifting and positive to the other person. Having people in our lives with a natural approach to interpersonal touching can help us to become more balanced in this area.

My story:

As a teenager when my mother was unwell I felt quite lost. An older man Harold, a friend of my boyfriend's family invited me out for a walk and a chat. I felt quite safe with him as he was married and also involved with my youth group. I enjoyed our chats.

One time he asked if I would mind if we linked each other on the walk, I didn't. Even though I had a great relationship with my dad we never really hugged or had any physical contact. Having that friendly tactile closeness to another 'father' figure was very important to me at the time. I felt as if I was accepted in a certain space of love and safety.

Incidentally, Harold was a school psychologist in another school and was very interested in what I was experiencing in my life as I had become quite spiritually-minded. Harold has since passed away but I am grateful that he asked about linking me, had he just started to link me without talking about it I think I would have been wondering what this was all about. I would not have felt as safe.

BRAIN TRAIN

To be affectionate

Over the coming weeks watch out for opportunities to make brief and respectful physical connections that uplift yourself and another.

CHAPTER FOUR

CHARACTER STRENGTHS

Building on our Character Strengths is an enjoyable route to success. Knowing each other's strengths enables us to work with, rather than against each other.

Character Strength

> Building on our strengths is more productive than focusing on our short-comings and inabilities.

In 1998 Martin Seligman with a number of other psychologists had become quite disillusioned by the often negative labelling and diagnosis of people with 'mind' problems.

GPs and psychiatrists consult a thick book called the DSM-V (Diagnostic and Statistic Manual of Mental Illness 5) which lists all the possible dysfunctional symptoms a person can have. Like any book of illnesses, once you start focusing on certain symptoms you suddenly feel that you have a variety of these yourself.

Of course it is important to know what is going on when we are unable to cope, and sometimes targeted medication can lighten the burden of psychological problems. But we also know that many drugs have debilitating side effects.

Professor Seligman and his colleagues felt that too often a person's strengths and abilities are ignored in spite of research evidence that demonstrates, that successful people focus mainly on their strong points and develop those. When a person is left with a negative label it can become a disabling self-fulfilling focus on what is wrong, forgetting that there is so much more to life and who we are, than our problems.

A Book of Strengths

Positive psychologists [1 & 2] decided to investigate different cultures[3], altruistic societies and religious traditions to see if by chance there was a universal agreement about certain behaviours and attitudes, that we all appreciate as strengths in one another. Valuable qualities that we would wish to have and pass on to the next generation.

It turns out that there are a number of qualities which are recognised, not just in Western society but right across the world, as being admirable and well worth pursuing.

> Each one of us has character strengths which can energise us and help to improve other areas of our lives.

The Inuit people in Greenland, the Masai Tribes in Africa, various religions and societies, college students in America[4] and ancient philosophical writings all agreed that there are a number of specific qualities, that are well worth pursuing for a life of meaning and well-being for oneself and others.

Everyone agreed that certain human qualities are very special because these qualities or CHARACTER STRENGTHS are

Strengths that contribute to a
good life for oneself and others

Strengths that inspire
admiration rather than jealousy

Strengths that remain constant -
even when one's environment
and feelings change

On gathering the research from various places in the world Seligman and Peterson found that all these appreciated character strengths could be divided into six different categories[1]:

1. The WISDOM or MIND category
Welcoming new information, loving to learn, being open-minded towards others, being creative and original.

2. The COURAGE category:

Emotional strengths including perseverance in reaching for goals, being loyal to principles in spite of opposition and being true to oneself.

3. The HUMANITY/ RELATIONSHIP category:

These interpersonal strengths include being kind, loving and inclusive towards others and helping those who suffer.

4. The JUSTICE category:

These community strengths include fairness, being a team player, leading others in projects to create a better society for everyone and standing up for those less privileged.

5. The TEMPERANCE category:

These self-control strengths include an ability to stand back and work for long-term goals, being in control of one's negative emotions and not over-indulging in pleasures.

6. The TRANSCENDENCE category:

These spirituality strengths include gratitude, hope, seeing a deeper purpose, a non-materialistic view of the world and an awareness of a bigger picture.

Some cultures or traditions prioritise one category over another[4 & 5] but there is still an agreement across mankind that all the above qualities contribute to a better world. Developing character strengths leads to personal well-being provided one keeps a balance[5].

Too much of a strength can become a weakness.

> While self-discipline is necessary and admirable it has to be tempered with self-kindness and with a respectful acceptance of those who might approach life differently.

Religious institutions often encourage self-discipline and loyalty, as this helps to create a respectful environment with faith and modesty, and of goodness towards each other. However a certain amount of negative fundamentalism can creep in where one judges those outside of the group as villains. Those who break the rules can be viewed as infidels of lesser value and perhaps worthy of punishment. This can happen when the self-discipline strengths are valued above respect and common courtesy.

Learning to empathise

Getting to know these universal strengths can be a great

help to understanding other people better. Even though we may embody a number of well-being strengths it seems that each one of us is gifted with a particular set of strengths which makes us view life from that perspective.

The person who is **open-minded** and **loves to learn** would tend to study all the angles of a situation before deciding what to do. The person who has **justice strengths** however might make an immediate judgement of anything that seems to interfere with a person's human rights. Both parties could be right, but as they might approach the situation with different strengths and different priorities they might think, that the other person is on the wrong track.

A mature person however will realise that these are opportunities to learn from each other. Sometimes a quick decision is needed and at other times it is good to investigate all sides to find the right course of action.

Sometimes our focus can be quite narrow. We can be quick to feel that someone deliberately upsets our plans or stands in our way, when in reality they are simply coming from a different strength category.

We can make quite a fool of ourselves by trying to change somebody who comes from a very different strength category.

Knowing the six strength categories can help us to avoid hurtful confrontations. When we realise that someone else approaches the situation from a different strength category than our own, we can step back and create a space of negotiation.

> The challenge is to extend our empathy to a wider circle including those we do not know or understand.

Maybe we cannot change things but we can learn to empathise with one another even if we do not agree or cannot give others what they want. We can activate the 'mirror' neurons in our brain.

'Mirror' neurons help us to put ourselves into another person's position. This is similar to when we view a sports game and find ourselves getting so involved that we try to kick the ball into goal or shout instructions to a player even though we are sitting at home on the sofa and nobody can hear us.

We do it all the time with those we love; we put ourselves in their position and offer them a cup of tea, a helping hand or an approving look according to what we perceive them to feel and need.

Discover Your Personal Strengths

In some workplaces time is set aside to ask individuals when they feel they are at their best[6 & 7].

Similarly, we can ask ourselves what we most enjoy about our lives. Answer the following questions (use the six strength categories on pages 110/111 as inspiration):

What are you doing when your life is going really well?

....

....

....

....

What strengths are you using?

....

....

....

....

How could you use these strengths even more?

....

....

....

....

Getting Up Close to
The Mind & Wisdom Category

GROUP 1
Mind & Wisdom Strengths

How a Mind Strength Becomes a Mind Weakness

The Mind and Wisdom Strengths create amazing artists, scientists, problem-solvers, explorers, adventures, professors and teachers in all fields of life. However, strengths need to be nurtured otherwise they remain dormant.

We need an environment which allows us to develop and experiment with various strengths. Also, it takes time to use our strengths well. The Mind and Wisdom Strengths can quickly be turned into weaknesses when:

Love of Learning becomes an excuse not to contribute to practical chores and survival needs.

Open-mindedness and Interest become excuses not to commit oneself to something or somebody.

Judgement and Critical Thinking become hurtful and un-appreciative towards other people.

Perspective becomes an excuse not to participate in ordinary living.

Creativity and Originality become self-centred and so involved that people around us feel side-lined.

BRAIN TRAIN

Dave is in his early twenties. He decided to leave home at 16 to finish school in the Irish language on a remote island on the West Coast of Ireland. He now lives in Spain teaching children and adults English and has recently started up a school using iPads rather than books for learning:

I have wanted to travel from a very young age. I can't count how many times I packed my suitcase and said 'I'm leaving'. I'd stay outside my house until 1 o'clock in the morning in the cold because I just wanted to travel. At the same time I'm very grateful that my parents moved from Dublin to the countryside because it stopped me getting involved with drugs; all I saw was green fields!

I like to explore boundaries. When I play video games I always try to see how far I can go outside the goals. Every day I hear of someone doing something I thought was impossible.

I used to get in such trouble. I felt I wasn't the way I was supposed to be, but I can see now that it is ok to be different. I'd talk a lot and others wouldn't, but this is what makes me the person I am now.

I am concerned about an educational system which does not allow time for self-expression. Many young people do not know what direction to take because they are doing what everyone else is doing; they are not experimenting and trying different directions.

I have a sense of urgency to do my part to make a change. I know I can make a change.

Reflecting on the five Mind & Wisdom Strengths on page 116 or 122 which ones would you think Dave is using and how:

One of the Mind and Wisdom Strengths Dave is using is...........................when he.......................

....

....

another is ....when he............................

....

....

He is also using.....................when he................

....

Strength from Difficult Circumstances

Sometimes a character strength is developed through difficult circumstances. We are torn out of our ordinary safe environment and challenged to cope with a foreign situation. We find ourselves having to access different parts of our personality.

My Story:

When I was fourteen years old our family moved to Norway for four years. In Denmark I had always been welcomed as the new interesting kid in the class. In Norway however I found myself standing on my own in the schoolyard. I was wearing my newly self-sown purple pants which I was proud of having created.

I was creative and different but I did not fit into either of the two cliques: one group were wearing expensive high-brand ski-jackets, designer jeans and YES-badges to join the European Union. The other group were dressed in alternative left-wing military jackets wearing NO-badges against joining the EU.

It was a painful experience not to fit into either group and not to experience any curiosity or interest in me as the new kid on the block. Only later on did I realise that the other students felt intimidated by me because I had jumped a class. Also, I got private Norwegian lessons with the principal of the school. His wife was Danish and he had made a special study of the difference between the Norwegian and Danish language which are quite alike yet subtly different.

On hindsight this whole experience taught me not to make a judgement unless I get to know people. It is often impossible to know exactly what is going on in people's lives unless we get to know them better and somehow put ourselves into their shoes.

As it turned out I found acceptance and friendship in a Youth Club where people of various nationalities got together to do drama, sing in choir and participate in adventurous Catholic youth camps. - And Norway found oil which enabled them to remain independent of the European Union!

Train Yourself in Mind & Wisdom Strengths

More details of the Mind and Wisdom Strengths:

**MIND &
WISDOM
STRENGTH**

LOVE OF LEARNING
You are open to new skills and information because you love to learn. You want to learn from your mistakes rather than feeling sorry for yourself. You are willing to learn no matter where and when.

**CREATIVITY &
ORIGINALITY**
You think or behave in an innovative and creative way that others might not have thought about. You bring about good results through your imaginative ways either directly or indirectly through the arts.

**JUDGEMENT &
CRITICAL THINKING**
You tend to gain a balanced view by not jumping to conclusions before making a decision. You make a risk assessment and also examine your needs and wants before acting on them. You view things objectively.

**OPEN-MINDEDNESS
& INTEREST**
Healthy curiosity can be learned from small children or animals who look without judging. They are interested in every point of view and not upset by irregularities or opposite opinions, it is all something to explore.

PERSPECTIVE
You have a wisdom and an understanding which help you to develop a balanced view and see things in the right context.
Other people might look to you to help solve their problems through your experience and ability to see the bigger picture.

BRAIN TRAIN +

Choose a character strength from the page opposite and during the week look out for an opportunity to use it.

Over the coming week I will focus on the Character Strength of...

I will take this opportunity to look out for opportunities to....

....

....

....

Example

I choose to focus on the Creativity and Originality Strength.
I will look out for ways to be creative in writing this book.

Take A Picture

To remind yourself take a picture with your mobile phone of the box explaining the chosen character strength, and set it as your pc background or homepage for the week.

This way you are constructing a brain pathway which can help make this strength part of your natural personality.

Getting Up Close to the Courage Category

GROUP 2
Courage Strengths

Courage Means
not Giving Up

The COURAGE strengths focus on having emotional strength especially when one feels timid and does not want to upset anybody or fear rejection.

This is about being truthful about who we are, what we know and what we love doing. It is about having the courage to become fully absorbed in what we do, and daring to have hope that we will succeed if we keep going.

> Many people give up, but courageous people keep going because they believe something is important.

Resistance and conflict are seen as challenges to be overcome rather than a sign of having to give up.

We might feel afraid of other people's reactions, of being laughed at or failing at whatever we feel strongly about but we keep going all the same because we believe this is what must be done. We believe that what we do is important enough and ignore 'silly' fears. We carry on because we believe we are working at making the world a better place.

When a Courage Strength
Becomes a Weakness

The Courage Strengths create great heroes who keep going when the rest of us have given up. Courage can also be more subtle in the hidden heroes who work away in the background doing their best to make this world a better place. These are people who every day chisel away at what they believe in, people who speak their mind in spite of opposition and rejection.

Courage Strengths can go too far. It is a matter of learning to keep a balance otherwise:

Courage and Bravery become an excuse to take unnecessary risks that put our own or other people's lives at risk for something that is not of any great benefit.

Honesty and Integrity become an excuse to say hurtful things to others, or showing up their superficiality.

Passion and Enthusiasm become so important that we brush others aside and ignore the needs of those close to us.

Stability and Diligence become stubbornness or a work obsession at the expense of other people's feelings and needs.

Christina's Dream

Christina Noble was bullied, sexually abused by her uncle and living in dire poverty as her father drank away all the housekeeping money. As a young person after surviving the loss of her mother, being separated from her siblings and sent to a horrific orphanage she became homeless living in Phoenix Park and was gang raped. She gave birth to a son who was taken from her. She went to England and married what turned out to be an abusive husband who threatened to kill her if she left him. She eventually escaped without her three children after psychiatrists finally believed that it was her husband who was the problem, not her.

Thankfully, she got a house and a job that could pay for the counselling that she needed. Her children one by one returned to her as they had all witnessed their father's cruelty towards her. She had a caring second marriage which helped her to heal but she never forgot the dreams she had during her previous abuse, of helping street children in Vietnam.

When her own children were grown she went to Vietnam with only enough money to stay in a hotel for a while. Little by little she made friends with some of the abandoned street children, she organised parties and swimming (to give them a chance to shower) and made them feel loved.

Christina kept searching for a way to help more permanently and linked up with the co-ordinator of an orphanage who gave her a building she could use to set up a dignified living and play space for the children. She approached businesses to get support and kept on begging for financial support until she got it, she would even sing in nightclubs to raise money. She kept repeating that these children deserved to be loved explaining that she herself had been like them when she was growing up. She had been picking up food from the street and she had taken to begging to survive.

Christina Noble has started more than 100 projects that help thousands of children each year to get homes with playground, medical support and education. She is an inspiration to all of us never to give up in spite of resistance, cruelty and opposition.

We all love the heroes in films who despite opposition keep their dream or vision alive. Nelson Mandela of course is another person who throughout his twenty seven years in prison believed that a co-operative white and black South Africa was possible. This is seen in the film 'Invictus'.

BRAIN TRAIN

Reflecting on the four Courage Strengths on pages 124 or 130 which ones would you think Christina is using and how:

One of the Courage Strength Christina is using is
............................when she.....................................
....
....

another is...................................when she................
....

She is also using..................................when she....
....

**Train Yourself in
the Courage Strengths:**

COURAGE STRENGTHS

PASSION & ENTHUSIASM

You tend to become absorbed and fully engaged in what you do. You have a sense of vocation and ability to lose self-awareness and merge with the task at hand. You feel inspired and look forward to engaging with challenges.

COURAGE & BRAVERY

You have the courage to act according to your convictions rather than other people's expectations. You may feel fearful but you face the day with courage no matter what. You are of good cheer through pain, humiliations or illnesses. You are bigger than these.

PERSEVERANCE & DILIGENCE

You carry out work carefully and diligently. You keep going when others give up. Once you commit to something you see it through to the end. You enjoy the work without obsessing on perfection. You are ambitious in the best sense.

HONESTY & INTEGRITY

You live your life in a sincere, transparent, truthful way committed to what you truly believe is important.
You speak the truth and you act according to your heart and mind.
You are genuine and you unknowingly remind others of this quality.

130

BRAIN TRAIN +

Choose a character strength from the the page opposite and during the week look out for an opportunity to use it.

Over the coming week I will focus on the Character Strength of...

I will take this opportunity to look out for opportunities to....

....

....

Example

I choose to focus on the Passion and Enthusiasm Strength.

I will look out for ways to forget myself and be all absorbed in what I do making sure it is something I truly believe in.

Take a Picture

To remind yourself take a picture with your mobile phone of the box explaining the chosen character strength, and set it as your pc background or homepage for the week.

This way you are facilitating a brain pathway which can help make this strength part of your natural personality.

Getting Up Close to
The Relationship Category

GROUP 3
Relationship Strengths

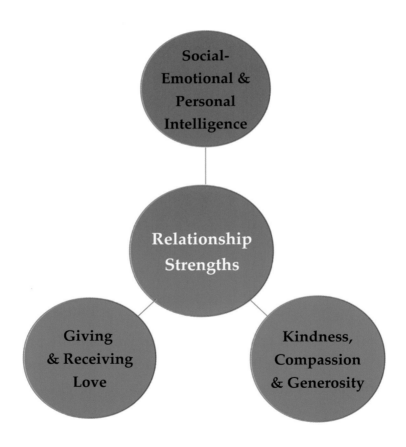

Relationship and Humanity Strengths

Social intelligence is the ability to tune into other people's feelings and respond accordingly but also to know one's own feelings and needs and be able to express them. It is about developing the best of one's abilities whilst also adapting to the needs of others around us.

Giving and receiving love through thoughtfulness and affectionate communication with people around us, is another humanity strength that we admire in others.

Relationship strengths are often called humanity strengths. Nurses and teachers frequently have these strengths. It consists in sharing resources and being caring without expecting something in return. It is about showing **compassion**.
Kindness is a fantastic strength that enables a person to give freely of their time and energy.

> It is about being vulnerable and open to share on a personal level, appreciating many types of love.

Humanity means respecting everyone whatever other people might say and being willing to affirm others in who they are, making them feel comfortable about themselves.

When Relationship Strengths become weaknesses:

Social-Emotional and Personal Intelligence strength goes too far when relationships become so important that one loses respect and turns one's back on anyone who does not have the same understanding of other people.

Giving and Receiving Love strength becomes a weakness when one starts pressuring others to return one's love, feeling a right to control other people's affections. It is a weakness when the love becomes so exclusive that only special people are accepted as worthy of love.

Kindness, Compassion and Generosity strengths have gone too far when one stops setting boundaries and condones people who act irresponsibly and disrespectfully. One can be compassionate without agreeing with someone's hurtful behaviour. One can be kind and still say 'no'.

Mother Teresa of Calcutta
had many relationship strengths.
She wanted the dying street children in
Calcutta to have a dignified death.
Although a principal of a posh school
elsewhere she could not stand back and do
nothing. She begged and begged until she
managed to start up a shelter where she
brought the dying from around Calcutta
to nurse them, give them food and
water and make them feel that
their lives were of value.

Danish girls Mette and her sister Lisa decided at an early age to save up money in order to volunteer in the Developing World. They saved their confirmation money and whatever money they earned from working in shops and nursing homes in their spare time. Over the past year they have spent 3 months in Tanzania. This is Mette's experience:

For me it started when I was learning about biology. I became convinced that I had to become a doctor. I thought I would go to Africa and work with Médecins Sans Frontières, MSF – Doctors who step into crisis situations around the world, independent of established organisations, and just help. Then I discovered that it was voluntary and that I couldn't make a living from it.

I decided that I would go and help voluntarily when I had finished school. My twin-sister and I saved up over five years; we set aside money every month. We both had jobs in our spare time. My sister wasn't that keen initially but I was going with or without her!

It is a combination of fascination with the workings of the body and being able to help others who don't know what is happening in their bodies. It was Africa perhaps because it was presented as the poorest part of the world.

It wasn't really about me being good or wanting to save somebody, it was about seeing others happy and being able to cause a smile on the face of children in the orphanage where we worked. I would highly recommend it as it puts our own daily lives into perspective.

Mette is now studying to become a doctor while her sister has gone back to Tanzania to support an AIDS project. They have a Facebook page where family and friends can donate to support the cause.

BRAIN TRAIN

Reflecting on the Relationship and Humanity Strengths on page 132 which ones would you think Mette is using and how:

One of the Relationship Strengths Mette is using

is ....when she...........................

....

and...when she....................

....

RELATIONSHIP STRENGTHS
(HUMANITY)

SOCIAL – EMOTIONAL & PERSONAL INTELLIGENCE

You have an ability to tune into other people's feelings and to respond accordingly.

You know your own feelings and needs and how to fulfil them in a healthy manner. This enables you to understand other people's needs and communicate compassionately and respectfully with them.

You know your own best qualities and find ways and places to develop and express these while adapting to the needs of others around you.

GIVING & RECEIVING LOVE

You have an affectionate nature and are thoughtful in your behaviour towards those close to you.

You allow yourself to be vulnerable and open to intimate sharing and caring.

You value receiving attention and are not afraid to commit yourself to deep sharing with another person as you appreciate love in all its aspects.

KINDNESS, COMPASSION & GENEROSITY

You enjoy giving freely of your time, you support others in their struggle for happiness and fulfilment. You share of your resources and give without expecting something in return. You help people feel very comfortable as you see them as equally worthy. You are respectful towards everyone no matter what other people might think or say.

138

BRAIN TRAIN +

Choose a character strength from the page opposite and during the week look out for an opportunity to use it.

Over the coming week I will focus on the Relationship Strength of...

I will take this opportunity to look out for opportunities to....

....

....

Example

I choose to focus on the Giving & Receiving Love Strength.

I will look out for ways to communicate in an encouraging and caring manner and of sharing my thoughts and feelings.

Take A Picture

To remind yourself of this task take a picture with your mobile phone of the box explaining the chosen character strength, and set it as your pc homepage or wallpaper on your mobile phone for a while.

Getting Up Close to
The Justice/Community Category

GROUP 4
Community Strengths

Social Responsibility, Loyalty & Team Work

Justice Strengths

Fairness & Equity

Leadership

Community and Justice Strengths

Civic or justice Strengths include **enjoying and partaking in community events** and concerns, and being willing to contribute to the well-being of mankind. A person might volunteer and support group goals without necessarily agreeing with everything.

The person who has a strong commitment to society and who is fiercely **loyal** to an authority will put in a lot of hours **without expecting any return** except the satisfaction of creating a more just world.

A person with a great **sense of fairness** and support allows everyone to fight for what they believe in and respects other people's goals.

A person with civic strengths might organise activities and **lead others** in the process whilst respecting everyone's point of view. If mistakes are made the person will admit it and learn from it thus inspiring others to do the same.

One acknowledges other people's contributions. No matter its size, it is viewed as equally valuable to the greater good.

When Justice and Community Strengths Go Astray

Social-Responsibility and Loyalty strengths become unhelpful when one starts defending people who are deliberately lazy and non-committal. Loyalty is an admirable strength but loyalty to someone who deliberately does not pull their weight is ill-placed.

Teamwork goes too far when one insists on deciding everything together when sometimes it is more practical to each have a particular responsibility and area of expertise.

Leadership strength has gone too far when one becomes bossy, bullying or aggressive and tries to control other people's lives.

Martin Luther King

Martin Luther King was another man who put his own life at risk to gain freedom for the black people in the U.S. Martin Luther King could not remain quiet when he saw how badly black people were treated. By being segregated and kept from equal opportunities of education and work the black people remained poor and humiliated.

King was assassinated which only increased the strength of his movement as people from all over the world rallied around to continue the work he had started. President Obama will most probably agree that had it not been for Martin Luther King and people like him he would never have been able to run for president and not to mention win the position, not once but twice.

L'Arche

When I was 18 I joined the l'Arche community in the north of France where volunteers from all over the world lived with those less privileged in society. L'Arche welcomed hundreds of institutionalised individuals with Down's Syndrome or learning challenges into small 'family' units to live a more dignified and normal life. It was inspiring to live in this community and care for these deeply wounded people.

One volunteer was a middle-aged Canadian woman Eliza who acted as secretary for the organisation. She slept in a tiny office on a thin mat which she rolled out every night from behind the shelves. She was the funniest, kindest person you could meet. Very few people were aware of her austere life-style.

The L'Arche organisation has communities all over the world. I stayed in one of those in Haiti as I wanted to make the world more just by helping people in the Developing countries. In the capital Port-au-Prince children with disabilities were often abandoned on the streets as their families felt incapable of coping with their special needs.

A local young man who had joined the small l'Arche

community helped run workshops in the poorest area of the town where people had to sit on stools all night when it rained, as the water washed through their humble dwellings made with corrugated roofing and straw. However I observed a lot of singing and drumming and friendliness in these beautiful people.

I have the greatest admiration for those who are committed to this work, even though my Scandinavian genes could not handle the humidity and heat.

BRAIN TRAIN

Reflecting on the Justice / Community Strengths on page 140 or 146 which ones would you notice in the volunteers in the l'Arche community :

One of the Community/Justice Strengths l'Arche volunteers are using is...
when they...
....

and...when
they...

JUSTICE
(COMMUNITY)
STRENGTHS

SOCIAL RESPONSIBILITY, LOYALTY & TEAMWORK

You partake in community events and causes.

You contribute selflessly for the good of society and value group goals even when they are different from your own.

You have a volunteering spirit and do not wait to be asked or told to do something.

You pull your weight fairly and with loyalty for the sake of the common goals of a team or group which you believe is worthwhile investing yourself in. You respect and work with authority.

LEADERSHIP

You have an ability to take responsibility and action in order to achieve a worthwhile goal and lead others in the process. You are able to organise activities whilst ensuring good relationships.

You are able to publicly admit to your mistakes and learn from them inspiring others to do better.

You endure set-backs and keep working for a better world.

FAIRNESS & EQUITY

You take care of your corner of the world and share whatever you can of your time, work and possessions to allow everyone to be happy. You give everyone a chance to fight for what they believe in and allow them to choose for themselves.

You expect everyone to be treated fairly and you do your best to acknowledge people's contributions however humble or great, it is all of equal value.

BRAIN TRAIN +

Choose a character strength from the page opposite and during the week look out for an opportunity to use it.

Over the coming week I will focus on the Justice Strength of..

I will take this opportunity to look out for opportunities to....

....

....

....

Example

I choose to focus on the Leadership Strength.

I will look out for ways of offering Positive Psychology Happiness Skills in schools - ways of inspiring others to help me as I believe everyone deserves to know these skills.

Take A Picture

To remind yourself of your chosen strength take a picture with your mobile phone of the box explaining it, and set it as a background on your phone or pc for a while.

Ghandi's commitment:

Mahatma Ghandi knew that Colonial authorities were treating the Indian people unfairly and he used the media to highlight this to the rest of the world, but he did it by committing himself to fasting and marching with the Indian people until he was listened to by the British authorities.

Gandhi led the Indian people to simply look for their fair share of work by organising non-violent opposition to the unfair treatment by the Colonials. These were shown up for their bullying methods used to suppress the people, and the rest of the world started to put pressure on Britain to return India to the Indian people.

While Gandhi
could have lived
his own prosperous life as a lawyer
he chose to give up personal security,
and campaign for the Indian people.

Richard Attenborough spend twelve
years campaigning for funds to make
the film 'Ghandi'
which shows some of this
amazing true story which has since
inspired people in every part
of the world.

Getting Up Close to
the Temperance Category

GROUP 5
Self-Control Strengths

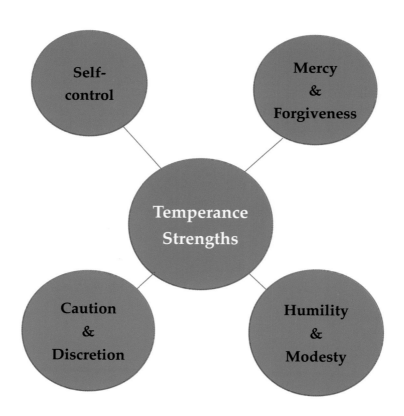

Healthy Habits

The temperance category focuses on the ability to take on and keep up healthy habits. While these strengths are less glamorous they protect us from a lot of dangers and help us to keep up habits that create good mental or physical health.

Caution enables us to calmly and respectfully negotiate a way through strong emotions and invite others to do the same.

Mercy and Forgiveness are signs of a bigger person who does not hold a grudge, who forgives and moves on.

Modesty and **Humility** help us not to become arrogant with success,

> Self-control helps us to keep working at our goals when we get to the uninteresting or difficult part of the job.

and to support others when they need a helping hand. We are happy for other people's success. We also know that at times we need forgiveness and mercy from others. We do not always get everything right.

Self-control enables a person to save up and to patiently work towards positive goals. It helps us to keep ourselves safe and not over-indulge in pleasures that will break down our health and well-being. It gives us the strength to say 'Thank you, but no, not for me', 'Not now'.

Temperance and Self-Control gone Out of Control

Self-control goes too far when a person does not allow themselves to enjoy food, good company, leisure time and is generally more concerned with being self-disciplined than getting on with other people.

Caution and Discretion is over the top when one stops taking calculated risks and trying new things. Hiding away one's talents instead of stepping out to improve the world around us is also a weakness rather than a strength.

Mercy and Forgiveness have gone too far when we stop people from experiencing the consequences of their choices, when we allow other people to keep hurting us.

Modesty and **Humility** are ill placed when we start putting ourselves down and make little of our contribution and ability to make a difference in this world.

Jack Kavanagh

I heard Jack Kavanagh speak from his wheelchair at a TEDx event in Dublin. Jack told us how he was a top-surfer and outdoors enthusiast until one day he miscalculated the depth of a wave and broke his neck when he dived in. He is paralysed from the neck down but through continual training and determination he now has limited use of his hands and arms.

The medical profession insists that he will never walk again but Jack is determined to defy that prediction. Every day he puts in hours of training to become more mobile. He can walk with the aid of a robotic suit.
www.youtube.com/watch?v=6yMSEF9x4hI

BRAIN TRAIN

Reflecting on the Temperance / Self-Control Strengths on page 150 or 156 which ones would you notice Jack using?

One of the Temperance/ Self-Control Strengths Jack is using is ....when he.................
....

My Dad

Although a brilliant student my dad Bent chose to become an apprentice in his uncle's hardware shop at the age of 14. He knew his parents were struggling financially so he declined their offer of support to continue school.

Throughout my childhood Dad held down a job in order to feed, clothe and house us children and my mum. When Mum started to suffer with psychotic episodes Dad studied psychology in order to understand her better. She continued to experience periods of psychosis and depression and never fully recovered.

When Mum later on got Parkinson's disease, Dad retired to mind her full-time even though he was then working as a fully qualified psychologist.

During Mum's last years dad was literally at her beck and call 24/7 but he always insists that he enjoyed caring for Mum. He always jokes that she never gave him a dull moment and admires how well she handled all her illnesses, something he believes he would not be able to cope with himself.

Through work Dad was able to get cigarettes and alcohol tax free, but he decided to give up smoking altogether even though he rarely smoked! Similarly, while Mum was in the psychiatric hospital he stopped drinking alcohol as he was afraid he would become too fond of it.

Dad is now 84 and still active. He enjoys supporting his lovely companion the best he can as she has a number of serious health issues.

BRAIN TRAIN

Reflecting on the various Temperance Strengths on page 150 or 156 would you notice some of those in my dad Bent's life?

One of the Temperance / Self-Control Strengths Bent used is ....when he.................

....

another is..when he...

....

TEMPERANCE
(SELF-CONTROL)
STRENGTHS

SELF-CONTROL

You have an ability to take on and maintain healthy habits rather than rushing into futile enjoyments.

You have the patience to look after your own mental, spiritual, emotional and physical health. You do not over-react when bad things happen but regulate your emotions in order to be helpful and calming towards others.

CAUTION & DISCRETION

You assess a situation before deciding or acting. You don't offer advice too readily but listen for all the facts and aim for long term results rather than rushing into something.

You know things can go wrong and take pre-cautions. You find ways of working around people's pride and other obstacles.

HUMILITY & MODESTY

You are aware of your own and other people's equality and oneness.

You do not boast of your achievement or interfere with others but allow people to find their way whilst attentive to lending a helping hand.

You do not see yourself as special and other people value your unpretentious contribution and support.

FORGIVENESS & MERCY

You make allowances for weakness and imperfection and are willing to give somebody more chances to get it right. You are able to let go of past hurts and allow them to transform you into a kinder and more tolerant person. You accept people's short-comings without allowing them to compromise your values.

Choose a character strength from the page opposite and during the week look out for an opportunity to use it.

Over the coming week I will focus on the Temperance Strength of..

I will take this opportunity to look out for opportunities to....
....
....
....

Example

I choose to focus on the Caution and Discretion Strength.

I will look out for moments to reflect before I speak as sometimes I am too direct or honest. I will delay a little to give myself time to answer in the most encouraging manner.

Take A Picture

To remind yourself of your chosen strength take a picture with your mobile phone of the box explaining it, and set it as your homepage on your mobile or pc for the week.

Getting Up Close to
The Transcendence Category

GROUP 6
Connecting to Something
Larger than Life

Connecting to Something
Larger than Life

While most people have an occasional **appreciation of beauty and excellence,** are **grateful and playful,** some people are particularly gifted in these areas. An appreciation of the gift of life or **being in awe** of creation and all its different nuances are transcendence strengths which can remind others that there is more to life than basic survival.

Being grateful for small ordinary experiences is a strength some people naturally possess while others might have to work for it. Chapter One explains the beneficial effects of gratitude, how it produces positive emotions and builds up our mental and physical health.

Having a sense of purpose and **belief that there is something bigger that connects us all**, and **sensing a spiritual presence within and around us** are other transcendence strengths which help us to a more holistic approach to life. Some people express this by participating in religious rituals or faith groups that bring people together in solidarity and love.

> Having trust in a loving caring God can bring peace and safety all around just like humour, laughter and playfulness lift the spirit.

When Transcendence Strengths go astray

Appreciating Beauty and Excellence goes astray when one becomes so picky that one will not accept something unless it is perfect or beautiful. Life has many facets and sometimes though it appears ugly or imperfect it may be a valuable part of something bigger.

Gratitude can become an excuse for not addressing things that need to be changed.

Spirituality, Faith and Religiousness go astray when they are used to pressure others to feel guilty or bad or used to think oneself better than others. Religion is counter productive when it is used to hold on to traditions that no longer make sense and when it is used to belittle ordinary people going about their business.

Playfulness and Humour go too far when one becomes sarcastic or hurtful towards others.

Hope can go astray when it becomes empty words of good wishes for others without doing something to help the situation when given the opportunity.

Francis story:

Francis has five children. Even though at one point he and his wife had no money and his business had gone bankrupt he kept believing that his children were given to him by God and therefore God would help him provide for the family.

All five children now have University Degrees and jobs that they love. Francis still does not have money but he has work and things happen which enable him to have a quality of life better than many people as he gets to travel a lot and spends quality time with his children and grandchildren.

BRAIN TRAIN

Reflecting on the various Transcendence Strengths on page 158 or 162 which would you notice Francis using?

One of the Transcendence Strengths Francis used was.. when he
....
....
another one was...................................when he
....

Christina Noble:

Christina Noble shares in her interviews and book her conviction that her experience of childhood abuse, rape and domestic violence prepared her for her work with the street children in Vietnam. She identifies with the thousands of abandoned children on the streets of Saigon as she herself was once that vulnerable due to poverty and homelessness. Christina does not regard herself as a traditional Catholic but she believes that God is helping her and guiding her in her work.

Moving on:

Irish woman Elber Twomey tells of her sorrow while on holiday in England when a suicidal taxi-driver drove into her car killing her unborn child, her 2-year old and her husband.

Every day Elber asks her 'heavenly army' to give her strength to get out of bed in the morning. She has found strength by moving from anger to compassion for the Polish suicidal driver who left behind a devastated widow. She lights candles for him.

Elber has also started a campaign to change the way the police handles suicidal drivers. She believed that the suicidal driver who purposely drove into the car was provoked by the police trying to flag him down. New training has now been implemented in the English police force on how to handle such volatile situations. Elber is also in negotiation with the Garda Training College in Ireland to create similar changes as her greatest wish is that what happened to her would never happen to anyone else.

BRAIN TRAIN

Reflecting on the various Transcendence Strengths on page 158 or 164 which would you notice Christina or Elber using?

One of the Transcendence Strengths.............
used is..
....
when she...
....
another is..
when she...

TRANSCENDENCE
(CONNECTING TO SOMETHING LARGER) STRENGTHS

APPRECIATION OF BEAUTY& EXCELLENCE

You appreciate everything as an amazing work of art. You have an ability to merge with art, nature, science. Even ordinary things give you a sense of awe and wonder. Observing human acts of goodness and courage elevates your spirit.

GRATITUDE

You appreciate the ever present miracle of life. You appreaciate others for who they are.
You do not take anything for granted and enjoy your surroundings wherever you are. You notice other people's contributions.

HOPE

You have goals and look forward to a better future.

PLAYFULNESS & HUMOUR

You do not take yourself or anyone else too seriously. You enjoy laughing and making other people smile at the marvellous experiences of life. You love having fun but not through cynicism.
You can be amused by the futility of your own importance as you choose to see the lighter side of life.

SPIRITUALITY, FAITH AND RELIGIOUSNESS

You have a sense of purpose and acceptance believing there is something beyond materialism and status. You have a connection with the Sacred which helps you to appreciate the vaste universe and the oneness of it all. You celebrate spirituality through religious rituals. You have an appreciation of God.

BRAIN TRAIN+

Choose a character strength from the page opposite and during the week look out for an opportunity to use it.

Over the coming week I will focus on the Transcendence Strength of..

I will take this opportunity to look out for chances to...............
....
....
....

Example

I choose to focus on the Playfulness and Humour Strength.
I will look out for ways to take myself less seriously and have a more humorous view of myself and my tendency to worry about what other people think.

Take A Picture

To remind yourself of this task take a picture with your mobile phone of a chosen character strength, and set it as your homepage on your pc or wallpaper on your phone for the week.

Applying the 5 to 1 Principle to Strengths

Character Strengths are a non-verbal universal language of encouragement and good will towards others. It is so easy to become shocked by or engrossed in our own or other people's weak points. Familiarising ourselves with a variety of strengths helps us to feel less threatened. We feel less defensive and stressed when we give our main attention to strengths rather than weaknesses. To overcome our negativity bias most of us need to up our strength focus to a 5 to 1 ratio of positive strengths to weaknesses. We do not want to ignore weaknesses but we want to keep them proportionate to their importance.

Up Your Strength Focus to a 5:1 through

1.   **Strength Cards**

2.   **Films, Stories, Song Lyrics and Interviews**[8]

3.   **Keeping a Strength Diary**

4.   **The Strength Game**

When schools include Character Strength teachings in the curriculum pupils become happier and more focused. This results in better grades and better relationships all around.

A positive focus on strengths pushes into the background the awareness of all the bad things happening in the world and gives us a more balanced view as most people are actually going about their lives trying their best to make a good life for themselves and others. We are each on a journey of discovery and development.

1. Strength Cards

Photocopy the 6 detailed strengths pages 122, 130, 138, 146, 156 and 164, and cut out the 24 cards. Alternatively get the cards online from www.HappinessSkills.ie

a) Choose 1 card as a theme for a week or a month

b) Google, Read and Talk about it

BRAIN TRAIN +

Join a speaking forum, debate theme or Toastmasters International where you always choose your own topic of speech

Example

I have chosen Originality and Creativity Strength. When I googled it I discovered that Originality is more about coming up with a number of ideas which may or may not be useful. Creativity is choosing particular ideas, working with them and presenting something personal to others.

As I sit here outside the McCauley Convent Tea Rooms on a sunny day I am inspired by the originality of this centre where people work voluntarily in the cafe. Behind it is a complex for the elderly. I am told there will be a game of bowls here tomorrow morning on the lawn in front of where I am sitting. There is originality all around this centre.

I think of Creativity and while the content of this book is not original I am delighted to present this material creatively, hopefully inspiring someone to make use of it to raise their happiness and well-being as I have.

2. Films, Stories, Song Lyrics and Interviews[8]

Once we open our eyes and ears we will be amazed by what we see and hear. We choose which films we watch, what music we listen to and which stories to read or pay attention to. To build your Strength Focus

a) Watch films with a main focus on good character strength and heroism

Many films have a main focus on good character with heroic strength in one form or another.

Example

Currently, I am following CSI: Cyber as I find it inspiring to watch a group of people dedicated to find and stop criminal hackers who use their skills for destruction. The 'heroes' of the program are good to one another and put their lives in danger in order to stop hurtful events in other people's lives. Even though it is fiction I am inspired by the community strengths and humanity strengths shown. Also I see the wisdom strengths used.

BRAIN TRAIN +

b) Listen to Music with uplifting lyrics that inspire positive strengths

There are many catchy tunes on You Tube, CDs, MP3 downloads, the radio and concerts. Choose music that expresses strength rather than weakness in order to raise your strength focus.

Example

I watched the Singer Imelda May TV series on Irish TV where she presented both accomplished and up-and-coming Artists in Ireland. Many of these have suffered for their art, perhaps been viewed as wasters or lazy. Many people do not view songwriting or music as a valid career unless one has already made it big.

I am currently inspired by the Irish group Kodaline even though I would not listen to all their music, but they talk about being true to themselves and writing from their own experience. This I believe takes courage and creativity and it is now paying off for them at last.

BRAIN TRAIN +

c) Read Stories that focus on Character Strengths rather than weakness

Example

I watched the film version of Eric Lomax's autobiography 'The Railway Man' with Colin Firth. Lomax was tortured in a Japanese prison camp but survived with severe Post Traumatic Stress Symptoms. Fortunately, later he met a wonderful woman who helped him to eventually face the perpetrator back in Japan. He had become convinced that he could only get him out of his mind if he killed him. However, Lomax ended up making a life-long friend of this 'converted' Japanese torturer who turned out to be a man deceived by his superiors.

Afterwards I decided to read the autobiography which was an amazing insight into how so many people were 'forgotten' in Japanese prison camps, were tortured, starved and abused. How Lomax and his colleagues survived is a miracle.

No-one is perfect, of course, that goes without saying but we choose what to focus on. Focusing on somebody's strengths does not mean that we allow them to boss us around or be disrespectful or take away from our well-being. Read more of this in the Assertiveness chapter.

3. Keeping a Strength Diary

In your PC, mobile phone or private notebook keep a Strength section where you write down how your chosen strength, or any strength, inspires you.

Keeping a diary of particularly impressive strengths experienced over the day or week helps to build up a long-term memory of goodness and care. This results in less defensiveness thus building up our immune system and freeing more creative forces within us.

Example

Today's entry in my Strength Dairy

I admire the originality and creativity (my chosen strength focus for a week) of the man who created this beautiful farm where I stay whilst writing this book.

No expense has been spared, yet it is not wasteful or showy. It is beautiful, functional and simple, yet one of a kind. I am inspired by observing somebody investing their fortune in a way that benefits not just their own family but also the surrounding area.

BRAIN TRAIN +

In the Family

Choose one of the 24 strengths as a theme for the month and create a card or poster that reminds everyone.

At dinner take turns to share how many times you spotted that strength in yourself or others over the day.

In School

Choose one of the 24 strengths as a monthly theme and highlight it in the school assembly or at the beginning of class discussing how this strength can be implemented in day-to-day situations.

Create a visual reminder of the strength

Storytelling
Sit in a circle and let everyone contribute a sentence at a time creating a story related to the monthly strength.

4. The Strength Game

The Strength Game consists in viewing a situation wearing a particular strength bias. The challenge is to explain what you would do in the given situation if you had the strength bias of a particular strength category.

For example

THE SITUATION: SHOPPING for dinner

BIAS 1: WISDOM STRENGTH (page 122)

If I was going shopping for dinner with wisdom strength I would probably explore a variety of new interesting goods before deciding which would be a wise buy. I might also suggest to the staff to stock an item I do not see on the shelves.

BIAS 2: COURAGE STRENGTH (page 130)

If I was going shopping for dinner with courage strength I would probably buy something healthy in line with my principles. I might ask the shop to get in something I believe will be of benefit like organic produce.

BIAS 3: RELATIONSHIP STRENGTH (page 138)

If I was going shopping for dinner with relationship strength I would probably look out for opportunities to greet people and have a chat. I would buy something I know others would enjoy.

BIAS 4: JUSTICE STRENGTH (page 146)

If I was going shopping for dinner with justice strength I would probably be concerned that the staff are getting fair wages, that Fair Trade products are promoted, and possibly talk to people to raise awareness of some community concern.

BIAS 5: SELF-DISCIPLINE STRENGTH (page 156)

If I was going shopping for dinner with self-discipline strength I might walk or cycle to the shop and have a small budget which I would stick to. No impulse buys!

BIAS 6: TRANSCENDENCE STRENGTH (page 164)

If I was shopping for dinner with transcendence I would be grateful, have fun and hope that everyone would be well.

The Strength game can be played in two ways:

A.   AS A CARD GAME

- cut out the 24 strengths from the previous 6 detailed pages explaining individual strengths in each category

- pick a card (without looking) and choose a situation from the list below. Everyone takes turns to explain how you would behave in that situation if you had a strength bias (from the card you pulled)

Complexity can be introduced by choosing several strengths

SITUATIONS (alternatively make up your own)
- **Spending your leisure time**
- **Choosing your dream job**
- **Planning a party or choosing a DVD**
- **Choosing mode of transport**
- **Finding perfect accommodation**

B.   USING THE STRENGTH TABLE -->>

Fill in the table on the right choosing a situation from above (or your own) and write or share with a group how you probably would behave according to each strength.
(TURN PAGE FOR EXAMPLE)

Having the Strength bias of:	Action When I ....I will:	Action When I ....I will:
1	**Wisdom strength of loving to learn,** being open-minded, creative and original.		
2	**Courage strength of strong principles** when others oppose me. I keep working for a better world.		
3	**Relationship values of** care, kindness, compassion and social intelligence.		
4	**Justice strengths of** leading a group to improve society for everyone. Fairness.		
5	**Self-control values of** humility and support to others. Feeling close to the earth.		
6	**Transcendence values** of gratitude, hope, faith, appreciation of beauty and excellence. Spirituality.		

	Having the Strength bias of:	Action When I am e.g. criticised I will:	Action When I ....I will:
1	**Wisdom strength of loving to learn,** being open-minded, creative and original.	try to learn from it, even if it is exaggerated	
2	**Courage strength, strong principles** when others oppose me. I keep working for a better world.	consider whether it helps me to do what I believe in or not	
3	**Relationship values of** care, kindness, compassion and social intelligence.	try to understand what is going on with that person	
4	**Justice strengths** leading a group to improve society for everyone. Fairness.	consider if their suggestion would help a greater good	
5	**Self-control values of** humility and support to others. Feeling close to the earth.	respect their point of view and possibly apologise	
6	**Transcendence values** of gratitude, hope, faith, appreciation of beauty and excellence. Spirituality.	thank the person for their interest then forget it, unless it is constructive	

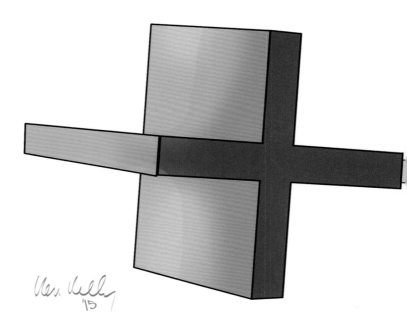

CHAPTER FIVE

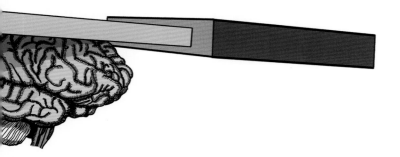

OPTIMISM SKILLS

Optimism skills can prevent and help to cure depression. When we spot our negative self-talk we can transform it into optimistic and encouraging predictions. There are simple ways of turning from pessimism towards optimism and hope.

Learning Optimism

One of the first optimism 'interventions' took place in an inner city school in the U.S. where a number of children were experiencing the onset of depression due to living in conflicted family situations. Their parents continually argued, often expressing hatred for one another in front of the children. These children experienced a mixture of sadness and shame, often blaming themselves for the parental conflict or break-up.

A team of positive psychologists put together an 'optimism' program to help these children combat depression and to help them cope with future difficulties[1 & 2]. The result was truly astonishing. Within a short time their mood lifted and they became happier and more outgoing.

> Even later on into their teens these 'optimism' children, previously at risk, experienced fewer difficulties and were better adjusted than their peers.

Regretfully, at-risk children without support adjust badly in their teen years. They may become addicted to alcohol or drugs, involved with criminality or develop a mental illness. But the learned 'teen optimists' were well and happy.

Optimism Skills

Optimism skills help us to change a negative outlook, and to interpret situations and challenges positively.
We replace the feeling of helplessness and negativity with a sense of control and joy.

> Optimistic people enjoy life more; they make adventurous and wise choices for themselves and others[2].

Excessive optimism can lead a person to

- over-indulge in alcohol, drugs, food, sex, shopping or entertainment

- ignore the bills that have to be paid

- ignore the devastating effect that over-doing something can have on the human body

- forget that our bodies need good nutrition, regular sleep and purposeful action for us to stay well.

Optimism and Our Will to Survive

Viktor Frankl[13] *is one of the few people who survived horrific treatment at Auschwitz, one of the cruelest German concentration camps set up during World War II. He could have escaped beforehand, but as a psychiatrist he was in charge of a mental hospital where he would write fake diagnoses for Jews who would otherwise have been executed. Also, he did not want to leave his ageing parents behind.*

Frankl, his wife and his parents were sent to a concentration camp where his dad died. His mother was murdered in the gas chamber. Frankl ended up in Auschwitz, not knowing whether his wife who was put into another camp was alive or dead. He was starving, frozen to the bone and forced to work hard for inhumane hours on end, as were his co-prisoners.

Previouly, Frankl had made quite a study of the human will to live. He had set up Youth Councils all over Europe where adolescents could get free advice. He was in charge of a 3000 bed female suicide hospital and was doing everything to help people find a meaningful life for themselves as he believed this would help to prevent suicide.

Frankl kept himself alive in the camps by thinking of and talking to the image of his wife; but he also wanted to survive to research why some people would want to take their own life and others would not.

He gathered a group of prisoners and told them to watch for when someone would be sitting staring aimlessly for hours, obviously having lost interest in living. The task then would be to help that individual to pinpoint something he wanted to do in the future after the camp, like for example talk to his grandchildren or tell others what had happened.

When a prisoner put his mind to believing that the war would be over by Easter, he would then have the strength to hang on, even though previously he had been ready to give up. However, when the war was not over by Easter, unless that man was able to say 'Okay, then perhaps by Christmas it will be all over', he would not survive. The prisoners learned to use optimism as a weapon for surviving inhuman conditions that would otherwise have killed them. Frankl lived until he was 92, having written books translated into 46 languages on meaningfulness and survival.

When someone dies, the person closest to them can lose interest in life. This can be a natural part of the grieving process but most people will eventually realise that a beloved can still live on within their memory. Sometimes, however, we can get stuck and need help to move on from the natural pessimism we experience due to the death of a loved one.

Negativity Bias - The Survival Instinct

We humans have a natural negativity bias as we remember negative events for much longer than positive events[3].

Martin Seligman and his team studied excessive and unhelpful negativity and pinpointed six specific ways that we undermine our own happiness:

We dramatize

We exaggerate an event to the extreme of disaster: 'This is the end of our world, everything is now lost!' or 'Everyone hates me'. Even if it was true, this is not a helpful way of thinking and most times we are totally wrong. Not everyone hates us. There is a positive side to the event, a lesson to learn. There are opportunities to communicate with other people. There is a survival story to tell afterwards.

We imagine we cannot
bear a particular discomfort or pain

We think we cannot cope with a particular situation or pain which is really bothering us, that this painful or unbearable situation will never stop; but it always does. We think an unbearable situation cannot be avoided in the future, but there are skills we can use and plans we can make to improve our future.

We keep imagining ourselves to be helpless

This is when we believe that we are no good at something and cannot learn even though we have never tried. Someone might have told us that someone else is brilliant (while we are not), but the truth is that our potential as human beings is enormous. If we were to set our minds to learn something or overcome some obstacle, we can link up with forces and people who will support that decision and help us to get to a place we never thought possible.

We believe something has to be perfect:

We think everything is lost because of one imperfect detail to which we keep giving attention. I get a spot on my dress, someone humiliates me publicly, I get a bump on my car, I don't reach that high note, I cannot get the nice colour I wanted for painting my walls, etc.

It is okay that we are not perfect.
It is okay that others are not perfect.
It is okay that jobs do not always get done perfectly due to time constraints and other priorities.

Life is full of imperfections and that is sometimes a painful experience.

Building our life expecting people to be well-behaved and things to work out perfectly to plan is bound to leave us disappointed most of the time. We need other priorities!

We see everything through a window of rejection:

When we feel life is not going too well for us we can start thinking and feeling that other people are looking down on us ignoring us or speaking about us behind our backs. Believing that other people are trying to deliberately harm us can be completely fabricated out of our imagination. Of course if somebody is bullying us or harming us we need to talk to them or someone else about this, but often this feeling of rejection can be based on something in our past.

Negative experiences from our past can colour how we view the world.

If we have had an experience of rejection from someone close and did not fully process it, unknown to ourselves we may have certain triggers or weak points. These pull us back into a darkened frame of mind. However, once we know this we can take steps to TURN our focus (see page 195).

> Most people tend to be more concerned about their own lives than ours. Even when they are mean or cruel, it has more to do with their inability to cope than with us.

Negative Conclusions
rarely come in ones!

Recently, I lost my car keys after parking and taking the train. When I eventually returned to my car, still without the keys, the passenger window had been smashed and some CDs were taken.

I observed myself moving through all the negativity conclusions:

*I thought I would never find the key (**dramatizing**) and that it would be almost impossible to get a new key.*

*I felt I could not handle not having a car (**pain intolerance**) as other people depended on me for lifts and I needed it for teaching in a town with no public transport.*

*I felt **totally helpless** as the key was nowhere to be found – it could be anywhere: on the train, on the street, in someone's pocket.*

*When I discovered the smashed car window **I felt rejected** – I could not have one evening out without something bad happening.*

*And I felt humiliated in front of my friend, as I had wanted a perfect evening (**perfectionism**), having got tickets for the River Dance show and organised a lovely trip by car and train to relax around the lovely Canal Theatre where the show was on.*

Thankfully, all along I recognised my negative assessments and kept making an effort to look for solutions rather than getting angry or depressed.

So many people helped me to look for the keys. A friend came in and brought us home. Everyone was super empathetic. The keys were found at the train-station, and we got a second hand car window at a reasonable price.

In the end really it was not that big a deal but only because I recognised the traps that were presented to me. Otherwise, I would have fallen apart. Someone else might be shaken by something entirely different.

Positive Illusions

> We might view ourselves as realists but research shows that realists tend to be slightly depressed.

We need a certain amount of positive illusions in order to believe that we can succeed and overcome future challenges[4].

People who are well and happy tend to use a slightly exaggerated form of optimism in crisis situations in order not to be overpowered by a negative experience or negative information. This works really well. Surprisingly, positive illusions are much closer to reality than we initially perceive due to our negativity bias.

Positive Illusions Gone Astray

Positive illusions can of course be so exaggerated that we become arrogant, thinking that we are indestructable, that we do not need to do the work required to succeed or do not need to consider other people's feelings.

Positive illusions have more to do with giving something a go rather than assuming that we just cannot do something. Most things can be learned.

How Do You Interpret

Failure

The **Optimist** looks at adversities or failures:

as a way of learning something new, a positive challenge:
'This happens to lots of people; they managed and so will I!'

as passing:
'Things will get back to normal or be even better'.

as only affecting one area of their life:
'Thankfully, I still have .... It could have been a lot worse.'

The **Pessimist** looks at adversities or failures:

as a personal rejection:
'I just cannot get anything right'

as permanent:
'Nothing ever works out for me.'

as a reflection on their whole life:
'This is disastrous. There is no point in making an effort'.

How Do You Interpret

Success

The **Optimist** looks at success:

as a personal encouragement:
'I am really getting places. I can make a difference!'

as permanent:
'It is great to have these skills in my back pocket'.

as affecting every area of their life:
'This is brilliant; my life is really coming together now'

The **Pessimist** looks at success:

as nothing important:
'Big deal! It was purely accidental, I am still nowhere'

as a once off:
'Sure that might never happen again'

as affecting a very small part of their life:
'It doesn't really make any difference. I am not much good'

Teach Yourself Optimism

Optimism skills help us to locate the negative thought patterns which rob us of happiness and life satisfaction. Here we make a conscious effort to locate negative thought-patterns and replace them with interpretations that lead to greater energy and hope.

There are a number of simple skills that lead to Optimism, to:

1. **TURN the event**
2. **SOFTEN your language**
3. **BUILD your self-optimism**
4. **SNAP into optimism**

1. TURN the event

Turning the negative experience or situation into a learning opportunity and personal advantage takes time. Brain pathways have been deepened over the years of spontaneously jumping to some negative conclusions.

What we want is to create new brain pathways that activate the feel-good hormones of dopamine and serotonin which open up our minds to creativity and hope rather than defensiveness and suspicion.

> An early negative event in life can have wired in a negative thought pattern.

Losing a parent or important person at an early age can leave a person with the impression that bad things are going to happen. Unless a person is supported in somehow processing the loss a negative world view can take root.

Similarly, when we grow up in a household where depression or violence is 'normal' we will tend to think that life is a difficult struggle rather than full of beautiful challenges to learn and enjoy.

Over time however we can turn things around. Positive words and affirmations and less absolute judgements can help us to create a different more helpful output[5]. Over time we can develop a trusting and positive mindset. There is everything to be gained by making the effort and nothing to lose by doing so - except our freedom to grumble and procrastinate.

BRAIN TRAIN
to TURN the table

The TURN Steps

TURNED is a well tested process which people use to literally turn a negative discouraging situation into a vision of positive potentiality. Based on the successful ABCDE[6] optimism programme that helped 8-year olds to process a discouraging and negative home-situation, TURN steps turn around potentially paralyzing experiences.

THE PROCESS

T	
U	
R	
N	
E	
D	

Place the word T-U-R-N-E-D vertically on an A4 page allowing space between each letter for the steps on the next page. (For a detailed template see www.HappinessSkills.ie).

	STEPS	YOUR STORY	MY STORY
T	**T**ell your story of this terrible traumatic or difficult situation you experienced		On entering a roundabout a car was 'suddenly' in front of me. I drove into it!
U	**U**nderstanding this to mean that ...		I am a terrible driver. I can't be trusted with a car It is going to cost a lot of money.
R	**R**esulting in which feelings, thoughts and mood for you?		I feel awful, a failure, a fool and frightened of being sued.
N	**N**ew nourishing approach, new attitude to this event:		No one was hurt. Only the side-door is damaged. My insurance is good. This is a valuable learning experience. Many other people made similar mistakes.

E	**Energy is now:**		More positive: a 'can do' approach. My mood has improved.
D	**Doing differently:**		I will drive with greater care, especially at roundabouts. I will consult with friends and the insurance company.

Turning our thoughts away from personal failure, from fearful future projections and money worries towards a self-compassionate and objective interpretation sets the mind free to cope.

Negative ruminations of disillusioned thoughts are broken and turned into constructive and connecting

Turning difficult and hurtful events to profitable personal experiences creates new optimistic brain pathways that help us to access helpful and healing thoughts in time of torment and disillusion.

thoughts that energise and inspire us to take the situation in our stride, sort it and move on.

TURN the table
at Home or in the Classroom

Holding an optimistic view of someone else can make all the difference. A number of longitudinal studies show that children and adolescents do much better academically and throughout life's various challenges when they experience someone who is optimistic on their behalf.

Using the above TURNED process is a reliable way of transforming our negativity bias into a more balanced and empowered position where we make healthy choices for ourselves and others.

Helping someone to TURN

Once familiar with the TURNed formula you can translate it into a friendly conversation whenever you feel someone is open to telling their story of misery:

T   **T**ell me what happened......

U   How are you **U**nderstanding this to affect your life?

R   The **R**esult of this is that you feel......

N   What would be a **N**ew **N**ourishing way of interpreting this situation?

E   How do you feel now? More in control? More **E**nergy?

D   What will you **D**o to benefit from this situation?

BRAIN TRAIN

Choose a situation from this list (or your own) and work your way through the TURN steps

- Lily's parents are always arguing and she feels it is her fault – **how could she TURN the experience?**

- Peter's dad is moving out as he wants to be with another woman and Peter feels betrayed –

- Jenny's sister had an accident and is now in a wheel-chair. Jenny is sad for her –

- Orlaigh's family is moving to another town on the other side of the country and she feels she will lose all her friends –

STEPS	YOUR STORIES		
T **Tell your terrible/ traumatic or difficult story**			
U **Present understanding of the situation**			

R **Resulting in which feelings, thoughts and mood?**			
N **New nourishing approach, new attitude to this event?**			
E **Energy is now?**			
D **What to do now?**			

2. Softening
your Statements[7]

> We may not be aware, but when we exaggerate and dramatise negative events we are priming our minds for a negative outcome, not just for now but also for the future.

Words like

- **ALWAYS**
- **NEVER**
- **NOTHING EVER**
- **NO ONE**
- **EVERYONE**
- **CAN'T**
- **WON'T**
- **I HATE**
- **I DON'T LIKE**
- **TOO DIFFICULT**

tell our minds to close off to certain people, possibilities and even to compassion for ourselves.

By being more accurate we will not get the satisfaction of being the victim in a big drama, but we might preserve a more truthful connection to other people and a genuine belief in ourselves.

By simply toning down extreme statements we programme ourselves for a more optimistic outcome.

BRAIN TRAIN

Watching Your Language

Pessimistic Language	Optimistic Language
ALWAYS	SOMETIMES
NEVER	FOR THE MOMENT BUT
NO ONE	Someone specific
EVERYONE	Someone specific
I CAN'T	I COULD LEARN
I HATE	I DON'T UNDERSTAND
I DON'T LIKE	I WONDER ABOUT
TOO difficult	CHALLENGING
S/HE HATES	S/HE DOESN'T LIKE or DOESN'T UNDERSTAND

When people close to you are dramatizing an event you can gently ask: *'Do you* mean....?' exchanging their pessimistic descriptions with a more optimistic version.

or ask *'Who exactly are you referring to?'*

The Railway Man discovered
the more optimistic explanation[14]

Eric Lomax, the railway expert who was tortured in Japanese prison camps, did not speak about his horrible experiences when he returned to England. The specific torturer Nagase was imprinted on his brain as he dreamt of a chance to get revenge on this man who had not been tried for his war crimes.

One day Lomax discovered that his former torturer was alive and getting publicity because he was running a centre of reconciliation and had become a Buddhist priest to make amends for his crimes.

Lomax doubted Nagase's sincerity as he had been so very cruel, not physically as he was 'only' the translator but psychologically. Over and over he had accused Lomax of lying and told him that he would be killed.

Lomax and his wife decided to raise money to go to Japan and meet Nagase; it was expensive as Lomax could only fly 1st class due to his war injuries.

When Lomax met Nagase he discovered that he also had nightmares due to witnessing Lomax being tortured. He felt extremely sorry for the part he had played and emphasised that it was only right that he should suffer for what he had done.

Lomax and Nagase talked through the whole incident and ended up becoming amazingly close friends, laughing and chatting together as Nagase and his wife explained to them the various projects they were involved with. One of these was to show young people how horrible war is and how wrong it had been to blindly obey the emperor and ignore human rights.

Lomax found healing in his discovery that Nagase also had suffered and was not such an evil man. He wrote Nagase a letter of forgiveness which meant the world to Nagase who had never been able to forgive himself for his own behaviour.

BRAIN TRAIN

Making the Switch

Using the Optimistic wording on page 205
translate the following pessimistic statements into
optimistic and hopeful statements.

(alone or in a group)

'I hate ....; she is always in a bad mood'

....

'I don't like ambulances'

....

'This job is too difficult'

....

'Everyone is laughing at me' - 'No one likes me'

....

'I never get to do anything interesting'

....

'I always fail at .... '

....

Notice how translating pessimism into optimism can lift your mood!

BRAIN TRAIN +

Invite a person (or yourself) to say:

'**I can't**' and
ask how that feels,
afterwards invite the person (or you) to say
'**I can**' and **ask if that feels different**

'**I don't know**'
and **ask how that feels,**
afterwards invite the person (or you) to say
'**I'll find out**' and then **ask if that feels different**

'**I can't do it**' and
ask how that feels
afterwards invite the person (or you) to say
'**I'll give it a go**' and **ask if that feels different**

BRAIN TRAIN ++

3. Self-Optimism

a) Practise reading and saying these positive affirmations[8], you can also listen to them on www.HappinessSkills.ie:

'It's ok to be upset sometimes, it's an opportunity to learn something about myself and my own feelings.'

'I get on with others; there may be upsets and mis-communications, but that's all part of learning about one another'

'I am a good person. I may make mistakes, but that's okay as long as I am willing to learn from them.'

'I am a capable person. I have special Character Strengths which I will continue to develop.'

'I can do!'

'I will do!'

'Life is good for me! And for others'

**b) Create and write out your personal affirmations.
Read them before you go asleep;
this will programme your brain to create positive brain
pathways.**

My positive affirmations

....

....

....

....

....

....

....

....

....

....

**c) Record your positive affirmations as a voice clip on your
mobile phone and then listen to it at any time, especially
before falling asleep.**

These activities create an alternative positive brain pathway
that little by little replaces the negative self-talk you might
habitually feed your brain.

Youth Crisis

Adolescents in spite of popular belief, actually take on their parents' attitudes much more than they realise. When parents use optimistic language they influence the rest of the family to do the same. Youth binge drinking and over-indulgences can often be linked to pessimism, due to an overload of negative information and a negative self-image.

We change our language to a more optimistic point of view when we read and listen to positive affirmations (samples included on www.HappinessSkills.ie).

Keeping positive affirmations beside our bed allows us to read them last thing at night or first thing in the morning.

BRAIN TRAIN +

4. Snapping into Optimism

Change pessimistic self-talk by wearing a rubber wristband.
(charities and businesses often give them away).
Each time you become aware of a negative, unhelpful thought snap the band as if to snap out of that frame of mind into a happier, optimistic way of thinking.

212

BRAIN TRAIN +++

5. Writing about Your Worst Experiences

We might think that we are better off forgetting negative bad experiences, but the psychologist James Pennebaker[9] found the opposite. He had serious difficulties in his marriage but discovered that journaling his feelings and thoughts helped him to clarify what he wanted and what he valued. He was convinced that this saved his marriage and initiated research to see if personal writing about feelings and thoughts within difficult situations was healing for other people too.

Pennebaker's research showed over and again that people who wrote for 20-30 minutes for four consecutive days about a trauma or negative event they had experienced earlier in life, remained healthier for much longer than people who simply wrote about general events or did not write at all.

Even though stories might start with a lot of anger, confusion and bitterness, they usually end on an optimistic note of having learned something valuable through the experience. Sometimes this is called Post Traumatic Growth[10].

How to Clear the Deck

We have all had some experiences which have felt deeply negative. This can keep affecting our way of interpreting other events as we expect failure or rejection. Writing about these events, however, can help clear the deck and to start over on a more optimistic note.

Individuals who followed these instructions all discovered some positive outcomes. We may have experienced great losses, but we might discover that we also gained something precious in the process.

GUIDELINES:

For three consecutive days write for 10-20 minutes per day about some personal difficulty in your life.

Keep writing even if you are repeating yourself and do not worry about spelling or grammer. This is just for you.

If you suddenly feel overly distressed, STOP and write about something less distressing.

Pennebaker in his researcch found that it can be normal to feel sad, angry and confused the first two days, then it will start lifting[11]: He stresses how traumatic experiences can be tied to childhood or relationship experiences with people who are important in our lives. But it does not have to be about a trauma. We all experience conflicts and stressful situations which we need to process and put into perspective.

A word of caution: When working with young people, it would be important to know them well enough to notice whether someone is getting overly distressed or unhappy and needs special attention. It can be useful to start with a less distressing incident.

Children are best helped through this process by writing stories that allow them to project their experience onto an animal character or imaginary person[12]. Try to locate your children's feelings around a problem and give them a sentence that will start them off.

HAPPINESS SKILLS

CHAPTER SIX

ASSERTIVENESS & FLOW

Immersing ourselves in something we love is healthy and life-changing. This however cannot happen unless we create personal boundaries to protect us and find non-violent ways of asserting our needs and aspirations.

217

Being in Flow
is Healthy

'Flow'[1] or 'Being in Flow' describes the ability to involve ourselves intensely with something we love doing. This is very healthy as it increases dopamine and serotonin activities in the brain, which fortifies our immune system and promotes optimism. Boredom and inactivity tend to produce anxiety which has the opposite effect.

> Flow describes the state of being all-absorbed and challenged to use many of the skills within our reach without it being so difficult that we cannot manage.

Living in Flow, loving what we do, at least some part of the day is important as we could otherwise tend to get defensive, or be jealous of other people who are fully engaged in what they do.

So Why
Don't We 'Flow'?

One reason for not living in flow is a fear of criticism and failure. Daily holding on to these fears, often unconsciously, produces unproductive stress which over time compromises our immune system. The stress hormone cortisol gets trapped in the body[2] due to inactivity and can shorten our life-span through cancerous growths, heart disease or general wear and tear on all the organs. Cortisol is good in small doses for sudden protection and strength to act, but it is unhelpful to live in a permanent state of arousal.

We Need Assertiveness to Live Happily

Many of us adjust our behaviour so as not to upset others and get into trouble. While this can be good as there must be give and take in every walk of life, taken too far it can be completely debilitating.

Individuals, who do not know how to protect their own selfhood or personality, who allow other people to dictate every part of their lives, often end up with physical[3] or mental difficulties[4]. Similarly being dominated by a bully is detrimental to our well-being.

Angela, a young mother explains how an unhealthy relationship dynamic took away her freedom to be herself.

When I was with my ex boy-friend he was very jealous so I changed who I was in order not to upset him. He didn't like me talking to other people.

It is only after the relationship was over that I realised how unhappy I was as I was unable to be myself. I became extremely moody and felt I was treading on egg-shells every time I talked to someone. I became very insecure around him, and then he doubted me even more.

People who are well and happy use a measured amount of assertiveness to empower themselves in their search for positive involvement and relationships. Being overly assertive and not caring about other people's feelings or thoughts alienates others but ignoring our own thoughts and feelings and running away from who we are is equally destructive.

Imelda started studying but found that she could not go on even though her grandmother insisted that she should:

I experienced a lot of negativity towards my decision to discontinue my studies. I had to continually ask myself 'which is most important, is it what is best for me? Or is it what others want me to do?' I felt I should stay on the course because my nanny had paid for it, but I wasn't getting anything out of it. I had no reason to stay.

I was taking the bus, walking for half an hour and then standing outside the college and crying my eyes out. I finally asked myself why I kept doing that. It is a weakness of mine not to trust my own judgement. So I stopped it. As it turned out I wasn't the only one who found it too difficult.

We might be naturally assertive in some areas of our lives but there are areas for most of us, where we need to create more space for what is important and meaningful to us, for what facilitates 'flow'.

Assertiveness and Courage

Being assertive involves courage because we are risking rejection and criticism. However, when we do overcome our fears and reveal our feelings and thoughts we might be pleasantly surprised by the positive reactions we get. Once we do not pressure others to think, feel or do what we do, most people will react positively and respect us. Most people, once given some time, will come around to, if not accepting, at least respecting our ideas and interests.

Taking Our Rightful Place

We tend to relax with people who know what they want and share what they think, while the silent unknown sometimes can feel threatening or confusing[5].

> We can be afraid of offending others with our pursuit of 'Flow' but people who are assertive about their goals and pursue their 'dreams' and are happy are more likeable and trusted by others.

Coaches, nurses[6] and bosses who, without being 'bossy', are assertive about letting people know what is expected, create more trust and get better results than unassertive quiet authority figures[7].

In order to pursue 'Flow' and develop our own skills and interests we will have to set up boundaries. We have to learn to say 'no' to certain activities or people in order to give enough time and attention to what we love.

Self-harm has been linked to a lack of assertiveness as this investigation shows:

> A group of women in Japan were in treatment for wrist-cutting. Many of these women revealed that they felt disempowered. Wrist-cutting was an attempt to gain some sense of control and release[8].

> However, fifteen minutes assertiveness training every second week over 1-4 years empowered these women:

> One of the women revealed how she had always sacrificed herself for others and went along with what others wanted. She learned to be calmly assertive and explain to others how she felt, especially to her mother who she sensed did not accept her for who she was. As she learned to be clearer about what she wanted she no longer felt a need to cut herself.

> Another woman in the group learned to stop criticising herself and to say 'no' to others in a respectful manner when she needed to do something for herself rather than for others.

Are you giving other people licence to ignore what you think, feel and want?[9]

By not speaking or standing up for what is important to us we give an impression of not having any particular thoughts, feelings or needs. Others tend to assume that we will want to go along with their plans, unless we tell them otherwise.

> Assertiveness is found somewhere in the middle between passivity and aggression: calm and kind, yet firm and direct.

There are ways of getting our message across.

Being aggressive about our personal needs or opinions only sidetracks the issue.

Even when our point of view is valid, loudness or negative outbursts result in other people not really hearing what we say. Most people interpret anger, irritation or whinging as an attack and will try to get away rather than relax and listen to what we are trying to say. Assertiveness however is respectful and kind.

Being clear about
what we want to say

It is not always easy to know what we feel or want. Assertiveness is linked to being comfortable connecting to one's own self as well as to other people. Processing our feelings and thoughts in a constructive manner enables us to clarify exactly, what it is we want and do not want. Researchers have found four dimensions of assertiveness:

○ To express positive feelings. Being able to give and receive praise and compliments[11].

○ To express one's opinion on something.

○ To be able to express negative feelings calmly and clearly such as defending one's rights in a public situation or withstanding peer pressure to over-indulge in alcohol, drugs or sex[10].

○ To express feelings of insecurity and inadequacy, acknowledging one's mistakes and coping with criticism. This sometimes involves asking for help.

Assertiveness
Tools

These are four ways of raising our Assertiveness and helping to increase our 'Flow':

1   **Create a Personal Space of Freedom**

2   **Keep Asking for What You Need**

3   **Receive and Divert Criticism**

4   **Make Requests in Your Personal Relationships**

BRAIN TRAIN

1   Create a Personal Space of Freedom

It is important to have boundaries around what is private and sacred to us otherwise we might find ourselves putting our lives on hold to cope with other people's demands. This is similar to leaving our door open and letting all the heat escape, or allowing anyone suddenly to walk in without notice.

We need to be clear on how much 'heat' we need to be comfortable, and how much privacy we need to feel safe.

When someone keeps demanding our attention and making suggestions on how we should behave and think we can be tempted to go along just for the sake of peace. While this is okay now and then, we need to focus on what is important and meaningful to us personally, otherwise we can end up not knowing who we are or what we want.

Many people stay helplessly disconnected from their real self because they do not take time and courage to build a strong fortress around their own safety and well-being. They allow authority figures or close family members to run their lives. This can be seriously damaging to their sense of freedom and well-being.

The sooner we take control of our personal well-being the healthier we will be and the more respect we will get for ourselves and others. We need to become our own best friend rather than being desperate to please others or measure up to other people's expectations.

> Our lives can be put on hold by a heightened sense of defensiveness, a negative interpretation of ourselves or a denial of our own needs[4].

Establish a Personal Boundary where You Feel Safe[4]

This is a mind/body visualization recommended by Terry Lynch, a GP in Limerick who has helped a number of people to restore a personal sense of safety and space.

BRAIN TRAIN

While standing, stretch out your arms and slowly turn full circle while **imagining a blue circle of light surrounding you** at arms length.

Imagine this blue light as **a protective shield** that stops you from getting hurt by other people's actions or words.

Place all the frustrating and confusing messages and people outside this shield.

You can still be kind but **you decide who you feel safe enough to allow inside your shield**.

Keep placing anything and anybody that makes you feel unsafe outside the circle and enjoy your chosen inner circle of freedom and love.

A guided 'SAFE SPACE' meditation can be downloaded and listened to on www.HappinessSkills.ie.

This visualization can be done several times a day to establish a personal space where one can befriend and mind oneself.

We are often much safer than we imagine ourselves to be.

We hear about the one plane that crashed and forget about the tens of thousands of planes landing safely. By choosing which information to allow inside our private circle we empower ourselves to not worry about events and people we cannot change.

Instead of focusing on the one criticism from someone we can 'rest' inside our safe circle in the memory of all the positive connections we have made over the past days with supportive people, nature, a pet, or the heroic deeds we have observed in inspiring films or stories.

Boundaries in the Family

Clear boundaries on what is allowed and what is not help everyone to feel safe, but allowing each other the personal space necessary to develop our personalities is also important. Children or young people who are less conformist because they have interests outside the societal mainstream may become victims of bullying unless they are helped to feel safe enough to be true to themselves.

Boundaries in the Classroom

Children do not learn when they feel threatened by criticism or are pressured to conform. Children with a weak sense of personal space are more open to being bullied. Guiding children through the Mind/Body Boundary visualization can help them to develop a greater sense of safety and assertiveness:

Have children spread out in the classroom so everyone can stretch out their arms and slowly turn around without touching anyone.

As you invite them to slowly turn with their arms outstretched guide them in imagining a blue circle of light all around them at arms length. See a sample script opposite.

SAMPLE MEDITATION SCRIPT

Inside your Imaginary Blue Circle you can learn to become your own friend. You can talk to yourself, think about life, about good things that happen.

You can push negative criticism of yourself outside the circle unless you think it is helpful.

You decide what and who to keep inside the circle, which friends are allowed in, who you feel safe with and who to keep at a distance.

Not that they are bad, not that you need to tell them, but you just know that right now you do not feel comfortable including them in your personal circle of peace and happiness. And that is okay.

If you wish you can connect with a loving Caring Creator who will look after you and mind you. You decide who you want near you, who you find supportive and caring.

Boundaries in Friendship

Having a sense of personal space and power is crucial to feeling safe enough to explore and learn about ourselves, what we love, what we think, what we feel and want.

Angela explains how she needs to be careful:

> *If I hang around with people on social welfare who are not doing anything to get work, then that becomes normal for me. I would lie in bed all day. I would go out with my friends in the evening, drive around the town and then go drinking.*

A good friend is someone who helps us to increase our sense of personal space. It is someone who respects us and encourages a positive way forward.

BRAIN TRAIN

2. To Know and Ask for What You Need

Feelings come and go so why is it important to know them and to express them? The problem is that we may act on our feelings but without knowing exactly why, or what we really feel. Acting on personal feelings without reflection can be damaging to ourselves and others; for example when we feel angry or disappointed and start blaming and trying to change other people's behaviour instead of discerning, what is really going on for ourselves. Knowing what we feel gives us the option of looking at our own needs, rather than trying to change what has happened.

BRAIN TRAIN

To Know
Your Feelings

By naming our particular feeling and examining the need/s behind it, we can learn to become more tuned in to what is going on within us. We gain control over a situation by realising what we need and then start expressing that to others.

My Feeling:

I feel...

....

....

(EG. I feel that my friend is gossiping about me behind my back, I feel hurt, angry and disappointed)

My Need/s:

I need ....

....

....

(EG.I need a friend I can trust, I need to feel loved and safe)

When I know my Needs
I can reflect on My Options:

One option would be to...

....

(EG. I can explain to my friend how I need to know I can trust her to keep my secrets)

Another option would be to ....

....

(EG. I could look out for someone else who I think might be more trustworthy)

A third possibility would be to...

....

....

(EG. I can make a decision to say nothing and give my friend a second chance to prove herself trustworthy as I could have misunderstood the situation)

There are a number of possible actions to take, but I might not be aware of these, until I take responsibility for my personal needs instead of expecting other people to know them, without me explaining or discussing it with them.

To Communicate Your Needs

When we learn to tune in to what is really going on within us and match this with specific needs, we can start looking for constructive ways of fulfilling those needs. Sometimes we can do it on our own, but often we need the support of other people for our needs to be fulfilled. Below are ways of getting other people onboard, whilst still respecting their feelings and needs.

When we express our needs we are setting an example to others, that it is okay to look for our needs to be fulfilled and it does not have to be by bullying or manipulating others. We invite and persuade, but respect the other person's freedom to refuse.

The 'Broken Record' Technique

The broken record technique is useful when something is important to us and we feel that others do not get this.

Sometimes a person in authority is not inclined to help us unless we specifically ask.

Sometimes a shop owner who has sold us faulty goods does not want to take them back or re-imburse us.

Sometimes a family member does not pull their weight

Sometimes a person holds on to something which we need.

When something is truly important to us, we need to do our best to persuade others to give us our fair due, both for their sake and ours.

The Broken Record technique consists in clarifying again and again what we would like, without nagging or turning aggressive or irritated.

When we repeat our request we do it as if we are doing it for the first time (no judgement).

Example:

*'I would like for us as a family
to find a way to go on holiday together'*
or
*'I would like to go away for a week
with a friend'*

Even though other family members do not seem keen, by repeating my request they will understand that this is important to me. On the other hand keeping quiet about this ensures, that nobody knows how much I would like this.

The BROKEN RECORD techniques would be most suited to situations where the other person does not really hear or acknowledge our request.

You might be amazed by how often people are willing to give you what you want, once you are clear and direct but friendly about it.

Keep repeating your request in an ever so friendly way. You are not scolding anyone or demanding, you are calmly stating what you would like, until you are satisfied that you have been heard.

How Important Is It to You?

To use the broken record technique, it is crucial to be sure that what we ask for is important to us, otherwise it might not be worth the energy it takes to keep asking for what we want, when someone tends to dismiss us. Once we know it is important, if necessary, we can write out a script beforehand and rehearse it.

Winning back a relationship

George Hook[14], a well-known radio presenter, reveals in his auto-biography how his wife was ready to leave him, but how he kept repeating that he loved her and that he would do anything to make the marriage work.

It took time but he convinced her by repeating this over and over and then doing what she asked of him.

BRAIN TRAIN

Role-playing:

Role-playing the Broken Record technique can be very helpful because we get an experience of what it is like to ask for what we want.

Here are **some situations** that can be **acted out with one another** (alternatively choose your own scenario):

- **Someone keeps using up all the milk**
- **Getting a refund in a shop**
- **Getting wages on time or getting a raise**
- **Getting someone to do the washing-up**
- **Getting a loan**
- **Pursuing an interest**
- **Getting money for something important**
- **Getting time off for personal reasons**

Person A makes the request while Person B plays the contrary but fair-minded opposition who is open to say 'yes' but reluctant to do so.

Afterwards **Swap Roles**.

In Friendship

A friend can help us to clarify whether a request is reasonable and important. Rehearsing the situation with a friend can prepare us better if we are not used to expressing to others what we would like or need.

2. Diverting Criticism

This technique comes into play when someone criticises us. Rather than defending ourselves we look for something we can agree with and then move on to what is more important.

CRITIC: You are always late, you don't care do you?

YOU: You're right I'm late. I'm very sorry. Now did you bring...

CRITIC: Don't try to change the subject

YOU: Sorry, I got caught in traffic, I should have left earlier. Now regarding that..... how far....?

It is not easy to agree with criticism as we tend to become defensive when someone is critical, especially when they exaggerate our shortcomings.
But rather than attacking the person we show that we are bigger than that.

It can be helpful to call to mind how some people can feel very irritated or have problems and take that out on us. Unless it is a close friend (turn to page 242 regarding assertiveness in a closer friendship) it is more helpful and energising to go with the flow and somehow agree with what we can, and then divert everyone's attention back to the work at hand.

BRAIN TRAIN

To Divert Criticism
Role-play in twos

Person A: criticises person B for one of the following:

- being arrogant
- bullying behaviour
- weakness
- selfishness
- telling tales or
- something of one's own choice

Person B: agrees as much as possible without losing dignity and then changes the topic of conversation to something interesting.

Afterwards: swap over and give B a chance to be criticised and finding something to agree with.

3. Assertiveness
in Closer Relationships

Honesty and open communication about what we feel and need in a relationship is crucial in building a supportive and positive relationship with each other.

> When we keep something important to ourselves for too long suddenly it may be blurted out in an inappropriate or hurtful manner.

When we keep all our needs and upsets to ourselves because we do not want to upset the other person or lose the relationship we might suddenly explode or implode.

The good news is that there is a wonderful, simple formula that creates a win/win situation. This formula has been taught in schools[12] and to US soldiers and their spouses. It has been widely proven to be of great value[13].

BRAIN TRAIN

To be Assertive
in Closer Relationships

1. Think about what you feel and what you want.

....

....

(EG. I feel other work is getting in the way of writing my book)

2. Ask humbly and directly (no blaming) for what you want.

I feel bad that .... *and I*
wonder if..

....

(EG. I feel bad that I am getting behind writing my book. I would like to get some time off to finish it.)

3. Take responsibility for your feelings and needs.

I know that ....*but I*
think if you could let me..

....

(EG. I know there is a lot of work here but I think I can catch up even if I take a few days to write my book.)

4. Repeat the request and explain how great it would be for you if the other person fulfilled that request.

I would really appreciate if you could let me...................................
.....................................*It would make a big difference to*
me..

(EG. It would mean a lot to me to take a few days off to finish my book. I will catch up with the chores when I return. Could you give me the three days off?)

If a relationship is good, more than likely the other person will respond positively or at least think about it.

If not, it may be time to have a chat about more underlying problems or revert to the Broken Record technique.

> *If the other person says 'Feeling bad is your problem!'*
> *You respond: 'I know feeling bad is my problem but I*
> *wonder would you be willing to help me to feel better*
> *by not ..... or by .....?'*

It can be difficult at first to change the habit of criticism and argument to an honest plea for kindness or consideration but it is well worth the effort and time as this creates a more caring bond between ourselves and the other person.

Assertiveness Gives Others a Chance of Knowing Us Better

If you want people to support you and get to know you it is important to speak up about what you need but in a way that invites good relationship and open communication between you and the other person. Asking for something does not always mean that we will get it, but at least we have asked and can move on. If it is really important we can either discuss it again or look for other ways of dealing with the situation and getting our needs met.

BRAIN TRAIN

In a Group or Classroom

Sometimes we assume that other people know what we need or feel, especially close friends or family, but mostly it is only when we articulate a need that other people really get it, even in close relationships.

In pairs role-play a situation using steps 1-4 on page 243. Alternate so both people get a chance to use the formula.

Sample situations:

- A friend is making noise that upsets me
- A friend borrows something without asking
- Someone keeps arguing
- Someone expects me to do their work
- Someone ignores me when we are in a bigger group
- I need help with some work/ someone to listen
- I need a new phone/ money for my phone

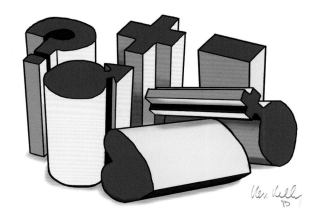

CHAPTER SEVEN

PROBLEM SOLVING

Personal or Social Problem-Solving concerns our ability to keep abreast of our personal and relationship problems. A build-up of these can have dire consequences on our mental and physical health, but there is a formula, there are solutions.

Personal
Problem-Solving

Problem-solving is often associated with business or mathematical skills but research provides ample evidence that good personal problem-solving skills increase our emotional intelligence[1], our confidence and our ability to be optimistic.

> Personal problem-solving has also been called Social Problem-Solving[2] because it concerns our ability to be in relationship with others, with the world around us and ourselves.

Some people will naturally possess these skills but they can be learned by all of us. There is a simple formula that has been observed in people who are successful at personal problem-solving.

Good problem-solving skills
tend to decrease depression, hopelessness
and suicidal tendencies[2].

People with depression, which we know is on the increase in our society, tend to have an overload of unsolved problems.

The human brain has a natural capacity to solve up-coming problems but it can happen that due to pessimistic thinking or lack of self-confidence that we limit our problem-solving capacity and do not work with our creative brain or struggle to carry out our solutions. It may not be our personal choice, but life can overwhelm us. We may not have people in our lives who know how to help us to solve our particular problems which then build up and hamper our well-being.

Eli 'the computer guy'[6] is a computer genius who makes free You Tube films to help anyone in business to improve their technical IT skills. He does so to help people to spend less time on technology and have higher earnings, which he would hope enables them to give more time and money to those in need!

Eli used to have nine people working for him but he ended up with a nervous break-down. He discovered how he needed to balance his technical 'geek' skills with outdoor activities, travelling and altruistic involvement.

Among other things Eli co-ordinates coastal rescue-teams. He sometimes shares part of his own story when he makes his You Tube instructional videos. This is what he shared concerning a period of depression he was experiencing:

'People like us 'geeks' who are paid to use our brains to set up or maintain business IT-systems can be more prone to depression because we often work alone and are under incredible pressure when something needs to be fixed or maintained. There might be no one else who can step in for us if we get sick or feel unwell. Your brain is your 'tool'.

I have found that when I feel this profound tiredness come on where I lose interest in everything and feel unable to cope, that is the time to PAUSE and make a plan. Even though it might upset other people it is better to pause for some weeks rather than keep going, burn out and not come back.

I find that many of my type of 'geek' people do not want to pause, they keep going and burn out. You have got to make a plan of what to do to mind yourself rather than ignore your discomfort. You have got to face it and decide what you need to do. Some people find medication helpful. I find travelling and doing something completely different for a while helps me to get out of that loss of energy and interest.'

SLEEP, A Wonderful Problem-Solver?

A good night's sleep or at least rest helps the brain to sort and 'file' a variety of under-lying personal problems but the unconscious brain can only deal with so much. If we try to avoid dealing with our problems and perhaps seek release through alcohol, drugs or loveless sexual behaviour our problems do not get solved.

We increase our problems through denying their existence and when we add unhelpful behaviour to these we multiply them. That is why personal problem-solving is such an important skill to learn early in life before we have too much of a build-up. We need to learn these simple skills that can help us to clarify what we experience, find suitable solutions and try to implement them the best we can.

Who to blame

The first step in facing our problems is to realise that this is not about blaming ourselves or others. It is about taking personal responsibility for our problems. We may not have brought them on ourselves and sometimes we cannot change a situation but we can always choose to change our attitude and decide how to proceed. We can choose a negative hopeless attitude or we can look for a way of viewing something that increases our well-being, energises us and restores our belief in life being a worth-while occupation.

Ciara experienced an accumulation of problems which resulted in her starting to self-harm, this is what she learned from it:

When I discover a problem I now take the time to think about why there is a problem rather than just freaking out. My mum is an innovative consultant so from her I've learned to look at things from outside the box.

For example when I have a headache, ok, I can take a pain-killer but I think for me problem-solving is a better solution. I write down the problem and break it down into more specific problems which I then tackle in different ways: I draw a spiderweb (brain map) of all the possible explanations for my headache, I could be stressed, I could be dehydrated, I could be sick. I try to find the root causes and then tackle these individually rather than making a rash decision to do something.

I would say to myself 'I need to fix this'. Breaking down a problem also helps to put it into perspective. Sometimes I worry 'Will I have enough time?' or 'Will I be ready in time' but when I look at it more closely I realise that this is not the end of the world; I can decide that next time I will do certain things differently. It is a learning process.

It doesn't always work but I think breaking a problem down puts things into perspective. If you rush into a problem and your brain/mind is racing you tend to freak out whereas when you take the time to stop and think of all the things associated with it, you will not frantically send emails to everyone but rather focus on the one person you need to talk to about it.

Stress and Health

We all have stressors in our lives. We decide whether to face our stressors face-on or try to escape them but in the long run facing these challenges is much more rewarding, and prevents future break-downs.

Below we see the flow of the feel-good hormones dopamine (blue) which helps us to feel motivated and persevere, and serotonin (red) which helps memory processing, mood enhancement, sleep and general good brain functioning that enables us to find good solutions to our problems[3].

Helpful hormones are activated when we take an optimistic 'can-do' approach even if initially we do not know the solution to our problems.

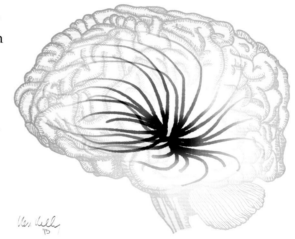

However, when we are negative or try to avoid our problems the brain freezes and our system goes into defence mode. This increases the flow of adrenalin and builds up cortisol. Our organs are now on the alert. When our system is on stand-by for fight, flight or freeze over time this can have a very depressing effect on our brain and body.

People who are stressed can also start suffering with a variety of physical or mental ailments such as heart disease, cancers, digestive problems[4] or mental difficulties. All these can be minimised by developing one's problem-solving skills.

Seamus, a composer, performer and audio-engineer was diagnosed with lymphoma which is a life-threatening cancer of the lymph-system. This is how his problem-solving skills helped him to try various solutions to deal with the pain he experienced before finally being diagnosed and treated:

I have an almost robotic approach; if there is something wrong with me I think: 'What is wrong?' and 'How do I fix it?'

I was sick for a long time. I did not know what was wrong, nobody knew. I was in a lot of pain and trying to figure out what that was. I went to Greece for a few weeks to organise a health holiday and the pain was not too bad but when I came back it got worse.

I studied fasting and fasted for 10 days, I tried a raw vegan diet, I tried re-bounding (jumping on a trampoline), skin-brushing and many other alternative health programs. None of them made any difference. I could not sleep and I was in too much pain to be flown to any foreign alternative health centre so I ended up in hospital.

When the doctor explained that it was lymphoma which is a form of cancer it was a shock. Seemingly lymphoma is very fast-growing and difficult to stop once it starts. I thought it might have been an appendix because my blood tests were perfect, I had been told I was in perfect health.

When the doctor said 'we have been in touch with the oncology department' it was as if he was saying 'we have been in touch with the execution chamber'. Within two days I was on chemo as they then knew exactly where it was and how to treat it.

I am not made of steel but I have this practical attitude that if I am meant to die I will, and there is nothing I can do about it. I suppose I would see dying as something positive, meeting God, and that I have to go some time. The environment was so supportive however, I remember one of the staff saying to me before one of my treatments 'You are a tough guy, you will get through it' and I got so much support when I came home. I could rest and get well.

More than likely the illness was caused by poisoning from various fumes I had been exposed to as a child and later from when I was shrink-wrapping CDs. Also I had been breathing in fungus fumes in my sound-studio which had been flooded and had no ventilation or sunlight.

Seamus has been clear of the cancer for over five years now but he is very careful around fumes and chemicals in his environment. He also eats five apricot kernels each day and makes sure to rest, where before he might have pushed himself beyond tiredness when he immersed himself in a project. And he is getting a new well-ventilated sound studio!

The DANCER
Problem-Solving Technique

One simple way of remembering the steps of the problem-solving process is through the **DANCER** formula which is based on ADAPT[5]. I like the idea of dance as we are trying to loosen up, yet learn particular steps which with practice make the dance so much easier. Turn over the page to see a visual version of this problem-solving template and examples:

D

Describe the problem(s)

Sometimes we have a number of problems all muddled together. By clearly describing individual problems we can go about processing them one by one.

A

Accept it as a positive challenge

Accept the problem(s) as a positive challenge which will have good solutions and teach you skills for future coping. Even if sometimes we cannot change the situation there and then, we can always accept it as a welcome learning experience which will stand to us later in life.

N

Name numerous possible solutions

This is where Brainstorming comes in. Brainstorming is to open ourselves to a variety of solutions without choosing which ones to go with. Alone or with someone we trust we allow ourselves to think outside the box. Crazy ideas are welcomed as sometimes good ideas come out of the unexpected. We write all of them down before we take the next step of assessing which one/s is/are most suitable. Creating a mind map or spiderweb as shown on page 262 can be helpful.

C

Compare the plus and minus sides of each solution & Choose

Predict the consequences of the possible solutions. Sometimes it is a combination of a few solutions that might work best.

When we take each suggested solution from the Brainstorming mind map and assess its pros and cons, little by little a plan will emerge as we discover which are the realistic and likeable actions that we wish to take. The solution might involve getting other people onboard, developing a skill or doing something difficult.

E

Execute the favourite solution/s

By executing the most favourable solution we get a chance to see how well it works. We might set a time-limit in order to help ourselves to carry out the solution. The emphasis is on trying out the solution, as what we thought might work may not always be possible and that is ok.

Once we have executed a solution that does not work we might discover another one that will, if not, we can do more brainstorming. When something is an ongoing problem for a long time it might take time to get to the root of it. Sometimes the only way we get there is by trying different options.

The important thing is to execute the solution even if that solution is to wait for a while. At least, we know that we can relax and not worry about something because we have a plan ready to go.

R

Review how well the chosen solution worked and decide whether you need to choose another one or to brainstorm again in order to incorporate new unforeseen factors which you have since discovered.

BRAIN TRAIN

in handling your problems using the
DANCER Problem-Solving Template
(download from www.HappinessSkills.ie)

Describe the problem/s	1
	2
	3
	4
	5
Accept the problem/s as a positive	These problems are all good because...

Next

Tackle One Problem

Name numerous possible solutions (brainstorming) to the first problem

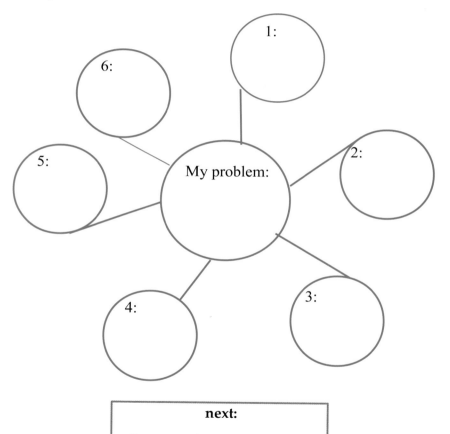

next:

Compare the plus and minus

sides of each solution

Choosing a solution		
As I assess the merit of each solution, the best one/s emerges		
SOLUTIONS	ADVANTAGES	DISADVANTAGES
1		
2		
3		
4		
5		
6		

next

Execute the favourite chosen solution/s:	
Who I need to help me:	
What I need to succeed:	

263

next

Review

When it will be done- (do I need to rehearse it?):	
When I will review and decide whether it worked or whether I need to have another go at solving it?	

DANCER Problem-Solving Example

Describe the problem/s	1 I feel horribly upset about everything
	2 My relationship with someone close is over
	3 I find no point in anything anymore
	4 No matter what I do it seems wrong
	5 There seems no point to anything
Accept the problem/s as a positive	All these problems are good, they do not feel good but there is a positive hopeful solution somewhere. It is not as bad as it feels.

Choosing One Problem at a Time

Naming numerous possible solutions (brainstorming) to the first problem

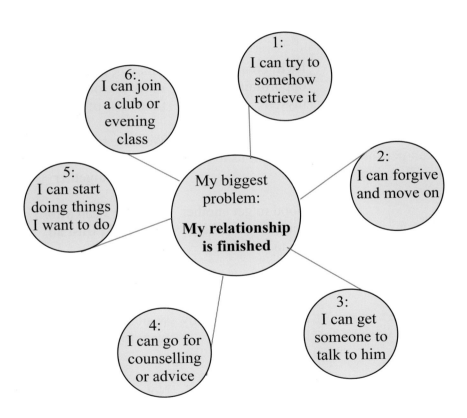

next

Comparing the plus and minus sides of each solution - then Choose a solution		
SOLUTIONS	ADVANTAGES	DISADVANTAGES
1 I can try to somehow retrieve the relationship	Maybe he still wants it, maybe I misunderstood	It wasn't really that good a relationship, he was mean
2 I can forgive and move on	I will create new opportunities for myself	I may not be able to move on, others may think less of me
3 I can get someone to talk to him	He might say sorry and want us to start over	We have tried so many times, we are not good together
4 I can go for counselling or advice	Good to get another point of view, help me to move on	Not sure I can afford it, or that I trust an outsider
5 I can start doing things I want to do	I would like to do so much more with my life-	I am not sure what I want to do and if I want to do it alone
6 I can join a club or an evening class	I could meet lots of interesting people and develop hobbies	Not sure I have the energy after work

Executing the favourite chosen solution/s:	Best to forgive and let go, he would have to earn another chance. Time to move on. I will start looking at interests that will energise me and give me a new start.
Who I need to help me:	I will speak with my friend .... and my dad, he is usually encouraging. I will go on the net to assess my character strengths and get involved with something.
What I need to succeed:	I need to believe that this is a chance for me to start over and develop new sides of myself. That I can manage without a relationship and that I will find someone more suitable.

next

Reviewing

When it will be done- (do I need to rehearse it?):	I will spend 10 minutes every day researching my character strengths and interests. I will write down affirmations today on my ability to move on and place them beside my bed.
When I will review and decide whether it worked or whether I need to have another go at solving it?	I will review in one week and see how I am getting on then.

Problem-Solving in the Family

My Story

My siblings and I were born within six and a half year which resulted in my parents having five of us children to organise. My dad being a military man however and my mum, although previous unfamiliar with cooking and housework came up with a plan to organise us little people.

Every Saturday afternoon we would have a family council. One of us would be secretary, another chairman and another in charge of buying the goodies for this get-together.

At these meetings we would listen to, discuss and comment on our parent's various proposals:

Pocket money would be according to age, thus there would be a small raise every year. We would be expected to have our rooms tidied before tea time every day. In addition we would get extra money for doing extra house-chores like polishing silverware and bronze ornaments (which we all hated) and hoovering.

If we saved for something my parents would supply the second half. I saved for a bike, a study table and a fabulous IKEA sofa bed.

Bedtime was according to age, an extra 15 minutes for each year, thus we were slightly staggered using the bathroom.

If we didn't smoke until we were 18 year old my parents would pay for the 20+ hours driving instruction that the Danish state requires for someone to get a driver's licence.

If we did not eat sweets during the week the reward was one krone each for fruit every Saturday. We five children would put our reward together and buy a box of grapes, apples, oranges or pears which we separate into five exactly equally sized portions!

These were great 'problem-solvers'. Another plan my parents put in place was the 'penalty-box'. We would be fined for being cheeky with mum, not tidying our rooms, ignoring a house duty or using swear words. It was only small fines but it all added up to pay for goodies for the Saturday family meeting (ice-cream and crisps).

To this day all my siblings are 'can-do' people, very involved in either their own business or the caring services and extremely devoted to their families. If there is a problem we siblings would be there either economically or emotionally for one another, so would our dad who thankfully is still around.

Problem-Solving
in a group / Class room

Positive Problem-Solving using the DANCER technique can be good fun as a group brainstorms together for various solutions to a problem and looks at the pros and cons for each solution and then make a plan of execution of the chosen solution. This can then be shared with the bigger group afterwards.

The problem situation can be real or imaginary depending on the relationship of the group. When a person feels safe among friends a real problem can bond a group as each contributes to help solve a shared or personal problem of a participant.

BRAIN TRAIN

In groups of two or three choose one of these imaginary situations (or your own) and apply the DANCER technique (Describe, Accept, Name numerous solutions, Compare and choose, Execute and Review). Afterwards, share with the bigger group:

- **You feel bullied because you are not into sports**
- **Your family is arguing all the time and you hate it**

- **Your alcohol consumption is getting out of hand**
- **You are hanging out with a negative bordering on violent group but you are afraid of leaving it**
- **You have fallen out with a close family member and you feel there is no way of reconciling**

Problem-Solving
in the Business World

Ciera's mum facilitates problem-solving professionally in corporations:

She goes into different companies and helps the company to look at a problem from various perspectives. When the problems within the company have been voiced and people feel safe enough to brainstorm around them, everyone seems to communicate better. It becomes clear that just because people do not agree it does not mean they cannot get on with one another.

When people gather to tackle a problem they start connecting with each other. They come out realising that together they can solve problems. They learn 'out of the box' thinking which helps them to better deal with future problems.

The Author's Final Word

Dear Reader,

Thank you for taking an interest in these Happiness and Well-being skills which mean everything to me. This is an invitation to take greater responsibility for your own life. Your mind, your time and your focus, you decide where to invest these and what to prioritise. You have the power to create a beautiful life for yourself and others.

I have had the privilege to share with you the following happiness and well-being skills based on positive psychology:

The positive emotion skills which are developed through focusing on the good events in your life and allowing yourself to experience their full impact.

The necessity for you to nurture yourself and to self-encourage. Learning to 'self-hug' and forgive yourself so as to better connect with yourself and the surrounding world.

The value of positive relationships and connecting positively with people in your surroundings. The ratio of 5:1 of positive to negative communications that creates lasting relationships.

A chance to appreciate the various character strengths so as to empathise fully with people who choose different priorities. Encouragement to be more of who you truly are.

The TURN formula helping you to view negative events as somehow beneficial, and over time, precious learning experiences. Switching to a language of Optimism.

Assertiveness with kindness which enables you to share with strangers or loved ones what is important and precious. To know what you need and go for it!

The necessity to face and search for definite answers to your problems. Using the DANCER technique to open your mind to innumerable possibilities for a successful outcome.

Through the BRAIN TRAIN sections you have been given opportunities to practise these skills.

Through meditations and affirmations you can calm yourself and build a deeper connection to your truest self.

Through *shared stories* you have been given real-life examples of *inspirational people* using these skills.

May you persevere, be courageous and empowered.

Useful websites:

www.happinessskills.ie

www.happify.com

www.authentichappiness.sas.upenn.edu/

www.ted.com/talks on psychology

http://emmons.faculty.ucdavis.edu/

www.self-compassion.org

www.gratitude.ie

NOTES

INTRODUCTION & CHAPTER 1: POSITIVE EMOTIONS AND GRATITUDE

1   Diener, E., & Biswas-Diener, R. (2008). *Rethinking happiness: The science of psychological wealth.* Malden, MA: Blackwell Publishing.
2   Fredrickson, Barbara (2009). *Positivity.* New York, NY: Crown
3   Lyubomirsky, S., King, L., & Diener, E. (2005). The Benefits of Frequent Positive Affect: Does Happiness Lead to Success? *Psychological Bulletin, 131*(6), 803-855. doi:10.1037/0033-2909.131.6.803
4   Davidson, Richard J. (2012). *The Emotional Life of the Brain.* London, UK: Hodder and Stoughton.
5   Hamilton, David (2010). *Why Kindness is good* London, UK: Hay House.
6   Emmons, Robert (2008). *Thanks. How Practising Gratitude Can Make You Happier.* New York, NY: Houghton Mifflin.
7   Fredrickson, B.L., Tugade, M.M., Waugh, C.E. & Larkin, G.R. (2003). What good are positive emotions in crises? A prospective study of resilience and emotions following the terrorist attacks on The United States on September 11, 2001. *Journal of Personality and Social Psychology.* 84(2), 365-376.
8   Emmons Lab, UCDavis, University of California (2011) Gratitude and Well-being. http://psychology.ucdavis.edu/Labs/emmons/PWT/index.cfm?Section=4
9   Seligman, M.E.P., Steen, T., Park, N., & Peterson, C. (2005). Positive psychology progress: Empirical validation of interventions. *American Psychologist*, 60(5), 410-
10 Algoe, S., Haidt, J., & Gable, S. (2008). Beyond reciprocity: Gratitude and relationships in everyday life. *Emotion*, 8, 425-429.
11 Seligman, M.E.P. (2011). *Flourish: A Visionary New Understanding of Happiness and Well-being.* New York, NY: Free Press.
12 Rash, J.A., Matsuba, M.K., & Prkachin, K.M. (2011). Gratitude and well-being: Who benefits the most from a gratitude intervention? *Applied Psychology: Health and Well-Being,* 3: 350-369.

CHAPTER 2: SELF-KINDNESS

1 Neff, K.D., Kirkpatrick, K., & Rude, S.S. (2007). Self-compassion and its link to adaptive psychological functioning. *Journal of Research in Personality, 41,* 908-916. doi: 10.1016/j.jrp.2006.08.002.
2 Longe, O., Maratos, F.A., Gilbert, P., Evans, G., Volker, F., Rockliff, H., & Rippon, G. (2010). Having a word with yourself: Neural correlates of self-criticism and self-reassurance. *NeuroImage, 49,* 1849-1856.   doi: 10.1016/j.neuroimage.2009.09.019
3 Hamilton, David (2010). *Why Kindness is good for you.* London, UK: Hay House.
4 Neff, K.D. (2011a). *Self-compassion. Stop beating yourself up and leave insecurity behind.* New York, NY: HarperCollins Publishers.
5 Rosenberg, M.B. (2003). *Non Violent Communication: A Language of Life.* Encinitas, CA: PuddleDancer Press
6 Williamsen, M.(1992) *A Return To Love: Reflections on the Principles of A Course in Miracles,* New York, NY: Harper Collins. From Chapter 7, Section 3, 190-191.
7 Hanson, R. & Mendius, R. (2009). *Buddha's Brain. The Practical Neuroscience of Happiness, Love and Wisdom.* Oakland, CA: New Harpinger Publications.
8 Cooperrider, D.L. & Whitney, D. (2005). *Appreciative Inquiry: A Positive Revolution in Change.* San Francisco, CA: Berrett-Koehler Pub.
9 Neff, K.D. (2011a). *Self-compassion. Stop beating yourself up and leave insecurity behind.* New York, NY: HarperCollins Publishers.

CHAPTER 3: POSIVE RELATIONSHIPS

1 Berscheid, E. (2003). 'The human's greatest strength: Other humans'. In Lisa G. Aspinwall & Ursula Staudinger (Eds): *A psychology of Human Strengths: Fundamental questions and future directions for a positive psychology.* Washington, DC: American Psychological Association *(*pp. 37-47).
2 Worcester Telegram & Gazette November 18, 1995. 'Rescuing hug' ,retrieved from http://www.planetdeb.net/spirit/rescue.htm
3 Bowlby, J. (1988). *A secure base.* New York, NY: Basic Books. Ben-Naim, S., Hirschberger, G., Ein-Dor, T., & Mikulincer, M. (2013). An Experimental Study of Emotion Regulation During Relationship Conflict Interactions: The Moderating Role of Attachment Orientations. *Emotion,* doi:10.1037/a0031473
4 Lyubomirsky, S. (2007). *The How of Happiness.* London, UK: Piatkus.
5 Werner, E.E. and Smith, R.S. *Overcoming the odds: High risk children from birth to adulthood.* Ithaca and London: Cornell University Press. 1992 (paperback 1994)
6 Noble, T. & McGrath, H. (2013). Well-being and resilience in young people and the role of positive relationships. In Sue Roffey (Ed.) *Positive relationships. Evidence Based Practice across the World.* London, UK: Springer (pg. 17-34)
7 Lyubomirsky, S. (2013). *The Myth of Happiness.* New York, NY: Penguin Press
8 Gottman, J.M. (1993). The roles of conflict engagement, escalation, and avoidance in marital interaction: A longitudinal view of five types of couples. *Journal of*

Consulting and Clinical Psychology, 61, 6-15.

9   Gaffney, M. (2011). *Flourishing.* Dublin, IRL: Penguin

10 Wang, M., Brinkworth, M., & Eccles, J. (2013). Moderating effects of teacher–student relationship in adolescent trajectories of emotional and behavioral adjustment. *Developmental Psychology, 49*(4), 690-705. doi:10.1037/a0027916

11 Lyubomirsky, S. (2013). *The Myth of Happiness.* New York, NY: Penguin Press
    Bonitz, V. (2008). Use of physical touch in the 'talking cure': A journey to the outskirts of psychotherapy. *Psychotherapy: Theory, Research, Practice, Training, 45*(3), 391-404. doi:10.1037/a0013311

12 Gable, S. L., Reis, H. T., Impett, E. A., & Asher, E. R. (2004). What Do You Do When Things Go Right? The Intrapersonal and Interpersonal Benefits of Sharing Positive Events. *Journal Of Personality And Social Psychology, 87*(2), 228-245. doi:10.1037/0022-3514.87.2.228

13 Frisch, M. (2005). *Quality of Life* Therapy. Hoboken, NJ: John Wiley & Sons

14 Harvey, JH & Omarzu, 1999, *Minding the close Relationship: A Theory of Relationship Enhancement,* New York: Combridge Uniersity Press

CHAPTER 4: CHARACTER STRENGTH

1   Peterson, C. & Seligman, M.E.P. (2004). *Character Strengths and Virtues.* New York: NY: Oxford University Press Ltd.

2   Dahlsgaard, K., Peterson, C., & Seligman, M. P. (2005). Shared Virtue: The Convergence of Valued Human Strengths Across Culture and History. *Review Of General Psychology, 9*(3), 203-213. doi:10.1037/1089-2680.9.3.203

3   Diener, E. & Biswas-Diener, R. (2008). *Happiness: Unlocking the Mysteries of Psychological Wealth.* Malden, MA: Blackwell Publishing.

4   Biswas-Diener, R. (2006). From the Equator to the North Pole: A study of Character Strengths. *Journal Of Happiness Studies, 7*(3), 293-310. doi:10.1007/s10902-005-3646-8

5   Satoshi, S., Otake, K., Park, N., Peterson, C., & Seligman, M. P. (2006). Convergence of Character Strengths in American and Japanese Young Adults. *Journal Of Happiness Studies, 7*(3), 311-322. doi:10.1007/s10902-005-3647-7

6   Linley, P., Nielsen, K. M., Wood, A. M., Gillett, R., & Biswas-Diener, R. (2010). Using signature strengths in pursuit of goals: Effects on goal progress, need satisfaction, and well-being, and implications for coaching psychologists. *International Coaching Psychology Review, 5*(1), 6-15.

7   Cooperrider, D.L. & Whitney, D. (2005). *Appreciative Inquiry: A Positive Revolution in Change.* San Francisco, CA: Berrett-Koehler Publishers.

8   Niemiec, R.M. & Wedding, D. (2008) *Positive Psychology at the Movies 2.* Boston, MA: Hogrefe Publishing.

CHAPTER 5: TURN TO OPTIMISM

1 Seligman, M.E.P., Reivich, K., Jaycox, L. & Gillham, J. (1995). *The Optimistic Child.* New York, NY: HarperPerennial.
2 Cunningham, E.G., Brandon, C.M. & Frydenberg, E. (2002) 'Enhancing Coping Resources in Early Adolescence through a school-based Program teaching Optimistic Thinking Skills', *Anxiety, Stress and Coping,* 15(4), pp.369-381.
3 Baumeister, R.F., Bratslavsky, E., Finkenauer, C. & Vohs, K.D. (2001). Bad is stronger than good. *Review of General Psychology, 5,* 323–370.
4 Taylor S, Armor D. Positive Illusions and Coping with Adversity. *Journal Of Personality* [serial online]. December 1996;64(4):873-898. Available from: SocINDEX with Full Text, Ipswich, MA. Accessed November 25, 2013.
5 Siegel, D. J. (2010). *Mindsight, the New Science of Personal Transformation.* New York, NY: Bantam Books
6 Seligman, M. (1992). *Learned Optimism: How to Change Your Mind and Your Life.* New York, NY: Pocket Books, Simon and Schuster Inc.
7 Burns, D. D. (1980). *Feeling Good. The New Mood Therapy, 1999 Edition.* New York, NY: First WholeCare
8 Kinnier, R. (2009). Attributions and affirmations for overcoming anxiety and depression. *Psychology & Psychotherapy: Theory, Research & Practice, 82*(2), 153-169.
9 Pennebaker, J. (1990). *Opening up: The Healing Power of Confiding in Others.* New York, NY: Morrow, Repr. *Opening Up: The Healing Power of Expressing Emotions.* New York: Guilford, 1997. ISBN 978-1-57230-238-9
10 Weiss, T & Berger, R. (2010). *Posttraumatic Growth and Culturally Competent Practice: Lessons Learned from Around the Globe.* Hoboken, NJ: John Wiley & Sons.
11 Gaschler, K. (2007). The Power of the Pen. *Scientific American Mind, 18*(4), 14-15.
12 Waters, T. (2008). The use of Therapeutic Storywriting Groups to support pupils with emotional difficulties. *Support For Learning,*(4), 187-192.
13 Frankl, V. (1959)*Man's Search for Meaning,* London, UK: Rider, Random House
14 Lomax, E.(1995) *The Railway Man,*London, UK: Vintage

CHAPTER SIX: FLOW AND ASSERTIVENESS

1 Chikszentmihalyi, M. (2002). *Flow, The classic work on how to achieve happiness.* London, UK: Rider
2 Lynge, B. (2007). *Anerkendende Paedagogik.* Copenhagen, DK: Bente Lynge og Dansk Psykologisk Forlag A/S
3 Hinnen, C. (2008). Relationship satisfaction in women: A longitudinal case-control study about the role of breast cancer, personal assertiveness, and partners' relationship-focused coping. *British Journal Of Health Psychology, 13*(4), 737-754.
4 Lynch, T. (2011). *Selfhood.* Limerick, IRL: Mental Health Publishing
5 Kilduff, G. J., & Galinsky, A. D. (2013). From the Ephemeral to the Enduring: How

Approach-Oriented Mindsets Lead to Greater Status. *Journal Of Personality & Social Psychology, 105*(5), 816-831. doi:10.1037/a0033667

6   Kukulu, K., Buldukoğlu, K., Kulakaç, Ö., & Köksal, C. (2006). THE EFFECTS OF LOCUS OF CONTROL, COMMUNICATION SKILLS AND SOCIAL SUPPORT ON ASSERTIVENESS IN FEMALE NURSING STUDENTS. *Social Behavior & Personality: An International Journal, 34*(1), 27-40.

7   ROTHERAM, M. (1982). VARIATIONS IN CHILDREN'S ASSERTIVENESS DUE TO TRAINER ASSERTION LEVEL.*Journal Of Community Psychology, 10*(3), 228-236.

8   Hayakawa, M. (2009). How Repeated 15-Minute Assertiveness Training Sessions Reduce Wrist Cutting In Patients with Borderline Personality Disorder. *American Journal Of Psychotherapy, 63*(1), 41-51.

9   Mayo Clinic Staff (17th June 2011). 'Being assertive: Reduce stress, communicate better'. Accessed from   www.mayoclinic.com

10   Goldberg-Lillehoj, C. J., Spoth, R., & Trudeau, L. (2005). Assertiveness Among Young Rural Adolescents: Relationship to Alcohol Use. *Journal Of Child & Adolescent Substance Abuse, 14*(3), 39-68. doi:10.1300/J029v14n03_03

11   Bekker, M. G. (2008). Predicting individual differences in autonomy-connectedness: the role of body awareness, alexithymia, and assertiveness. *Journal Of Clinical Psychology, 64*(6), 747-765.

12   Seligman, M.E.P., Reivich, K., Jaycox, L. & Gillham, J. (1995). *The Optimistic Child*. New York, NY: HarperPerennial.

13   Reivich, K.J., Seligman, M.E.P., & McBride, S. (2011). Master resilience training in the U.S. Army. *American Psychologist, 66* (25-34).

14   Hook, G. (2005) *Time Added On: Autobiography*, Ireland: Penguin

CHAPTER SEVEN: PROBLEM-SOLVING

1   Carr, A. (2004). *Positive Psychology. The Science of Happiness and Human Strengths*. New York, NY: Routledge.

2   Heppner, P. P. & Lee, D. (2005). Problem-solving appraisal and psychological adjustment in C. R. Snyder and S. J. Lopez (Eds.) *Handbook of Positive Psychology*. New York, NY: Oxford University Press.

3   Davidson, R. & Begley, S. (2012). *The Emotional Life of your Brain*. London, UK: Hodder and Stoughton Ltd.

4   D'Zurilla, T. J. & Nezu, A. M. (2007). *Problem-Solving Therapy. A Positive Approach to Clinical Intervention*. Third Edition. New York, NY: Springer Publ.

5   Washington, K. (2012). Qualitative evaluation of a problem-solving intervention for informal hospice caregivers. *Palliative Medicine, 26*(8), 1018-1024.

6   ELI the Computer Guy
    https://www.youtube.com/user/elithecomputerguy
    'Comment: Dealing with Depression as a Geek December 2014:

Index